HANOVER HARMONIES

The Musical Heritage of Hanover, PA

Ginger S. Myers

Pudlee Publishing Company

Manchester, Maryland

Published by

Pudlee Publishing Company
Post Office Box 895
Manchester, Maryland 21102
Telephone: (410) 374 - 1844
Facsimile (410) 239 - 1823

ISBN 0-9664263-0-4

This book is dedicated to all musicians that have lived their lives and made their music for the Glory of God. All else becomes as sounding brass or a tinkling cymbal.

Table of Contents

Acknowledgments

If it takes a village to raise a child, then it took a town to write this book. So many people in the Hanover area and beyond willing shared news clippings, pictures, and oral histories about Hanover's musical heritage with me, that without their input, this story would have remained untold. Although an extensive effort was made to glean information from every source available, it is conceivable that some group or individual may have been inadvertently missed in this chronicle. Also, groups who are relatively new to the music scene in Hanover were not detailed here. Such is the material of second editions.

Foremost, I want to thank my family for supporting me in completing this project. Their willingness to pick-up the slack at our house, allowed me time to do my research, struggle with my writing, and finally see this work in print.

I would like to thank the staff and volunteers of the Hanover Public Library for their assistance with my research. Without the volunteers who staff the Pennsylvania Room in the Hanover Public Library, the public would have only limited access to valuable historical data on a plethora of topics. I would like to thank Jean Martin, who allowed me access to photos and clippings in the St. Matthew Lutheran Church Archives and also Carolyn Stauffer, Director of the Hanover Historical Society, for sharing the society's collection with me.

A special thanks goes to Poist Studios. They reproduced all the photos in this book and even scanned their own archives for suitable negatives of past musical events. Their professionalism and courtesy added greatly to the visual acumen of this book.

The following persons provided me with material, pictures, oral histories, and when needed, a shoulder to lean on. Without them, this work would be incomplete. Thanks goes to Scott Fredericks, Nancy Leister, Mary Ann Fiery, Karen Buckwalter, Shirley Gobrecht Leister, Clair Hewitt, Larry Kuntz, Diane Hoffman, Jesse Betlyon, Paul Worchester, Robert Hartman, Bill Bowman, and Bob and Joel Menchey.

Getting Organized

It has long been an acknowledged fact that there is no town the size of Hanover or even with twice or three times its population which can boast of the musical ability, the number of expert musicians, and the number of different musical instruments manipulated by our people, two bands, which rank with the best anywhere, an orchestra and a drum corps, and numerous church musical societies. These facts are known. In addition to this, there are several hundred pianos, and more than that number of organs, used in the various homes of our town, together with numerous melodeons, harps, guitars, mandolins, violins, banjos, zithers, etc. This is a record, we will venture to say, that cannot be equaled or surpassed in any town with a population of 5000 in Pennsylvania or in the United States. Good for Hanover and its music-loving people."

Hanover Spectator Newspaper
March 31, 1892

A community can assess its character by how well its takes care of its young , the rank accorded to its elderly, the religious mores it embraces, the occupations its craftsmen pursue, and how its people spend their leisure time. Today, according to the US Census Bureau, Hanover, PA, is a scenic borough of over 40,000 people. Located on the edge of the largest metropolitan area in the country, it serves as a haven for those looking for the best of both worlds; somewhere that's a little bit city and still a little bit country. Blessed with an abundant water source and a skilled work force, by the outbreak of the Civil War, Hanover had established itself as a local commercial base. It was the strength of that commercial base that fueled the town's growth. It was the character of its townspeople that expanded its churches, built its schools and hospital, and fired its love for music.

Rogue's Harbor, Hickory Town, McAllister's Town; these were all earlier names for the same predominantly German settlement located on a tract of land purchased in 1745 by Richard McAllister. A Scotch Irishman of Presbyterian ancestry, McAllister had recently migrated to the Cumberland Valley. He laid out his purchase into lots and founded the town of Hanover, PA, in 1763.

However, Europeans had settled in the area prior to this date. The first whites into the area were Jesuit Priests, English and Scotch Irish, who located in the area in the late sixteen hundreds. German immigrants began to arrive at the settlement in 1727 and kindled much of its growth. It was during this period that the settlement took on its first name. Times were tempestuous and the name was born of the times; the locals called it Rogue's Harbor.

McAllister recognized that his destiny was strongly linked to the German Lutheran and Reformed settlers who had already built churches and trades in the area. He selected his town's name to appease them. According to the Hanover Centenniel Program printed in 1863,

> The project to build a town was amusing
> to some of the German settlers who first
> called it 'Hickory Town' because of the dense
> groves of hickory trees which grew

abundantly around. The name 'Hanover' was suggested by Michael Tanner, one of the commissioners who laid off York County in 1749 and who at this time owned large tracts of land southeast of the town. He was a native of Hannover, Germany, and in order to please the German settlers, the founder obeyed his suggestion, although the settlement was called 'McAllister's Town' for more than a third of a century.

It was the German settlers who were to make the defining mark on the emerging town's economic and cultural complexion. The Germans who settled west of the Susquehanna River were Palatines, German Baptists, and Mennonites. Those coming to the Hanover area in 1727 were mostly Palatines.

The Palatines were thrifty and industrious people who lived in the lower regions of the Rhine. Situated on both sides of the noble river, between Bavaria and Alsace, and extending from above the city of Speyer northward to near Cologne, the Palatine was as fair a land as all Europe could show... Religion and education were so well diffused that there were no other people of their day to whom in these respects the Palatines stood second. The situation of their native country, the highway from France into the heart of Germany, together with its beauty and fertility, made it a Naboth's vineyard to Louis XIV, whose ambition was colossal, whose absolutism could ill brook denial, and whose rapacity recoiled from no extreme cruelty. 1

It is needless to reiterate here the atrocities, starting in 1685, that were suffered by the Palatine people at the hands of Louis XIV and his grandson Philip, who used the region as a pawn in his fight to claim the Spanish crown. The region was in constant political and religious turmoil, making the lives of the largely Lutheran and Reform believers unbearable.

> At length in 1707, Louis dispatched an army to repeat, so far as possible, the rapines of twenty years before. With this, the cup of misery was full, and at once began the remarkable exodus, which in the next four decades brought so many thousands of Palatines to America." 2

The Palatines were a musical people by inheritance. They brought with them to the New World their German hymnals, folk songs, stringed instruments, fifes, drums, accordions, and an assortment of woodwind and brass instruments. Music was a soothing respite to a day's labor of clearing land, breaking ground, or tending a family.

Fife players and drummers from the Hanover area served in the Revolutionary War Corps with the famous Pennsylvania Line under the command of the impetuous Brig. Gen. "Mad" Anthony Wayne. The last surviving Hanoverian Revolutionary musician was George Blinsinger, a fife player, who died in the 1840's. His war-time fife was still in his possession at the time of his death.

Musical societies and clubs formed as the town settled into itself by the end of the eighteenth century. Francis Scott Key was born just 20 miles from Hanover in 1780. His

"Star-Spangled Banner" was sung for the first time in Hanover in the Center Square in 1836.

Local churches provided the earliest music meccas for the townsfolk; first with their choirs, then their bells, and then with their majestic organs. Ringing out their call to come to worship, the oldest twin church bells in the area are those of St. Matthew Lutheran Church.

According to St. Matthew's history, Nicholus Gelwicks and Peter Krumbine were instructed by the congregation in March 1807 to complete the church spire and secure tower bells for their newly completed church building. They were given a $65 salary each for their services and the privilege of having their names inscribed on the bells. The two bells were cast in Philadelphia. One bore the inscription, "Geo. H. Headerley cast us both in Philadelphia, in 1808'. The other was inscribed " Nicholus Gelwicks and Peter Krumbine".

The committee spent $1293.08 to complete the spire, one of the earliest examples of Christopher Wren architecture in the New World. The receipt for the bells, which is in the church's archives , shows the bells cost $569.40 They weighed 500 pounds each. They were transported down the Delaware River and the back up the Chesapeake Bay to Baltimore by barge and then traveled from the docks overland to Hanover in a six-horse drawn wagon owned by John Sholl . He was paid one pound and five shillings for the job. The total shipping costs were $45.58. Another $606.54 was spent in repairs to the church. The moneys needed to pay for the spire and the bells were raised, in part, by means of a lottery.

During the Battle of Hanover in 1863, General Judson Kilpatrick observed Confederate troop movements through his telescope while standing next to these bells in the old church spire. Today, the same bells call the faithful to worship each Sunday. The twin bells of St. Matthew's Lutheran Church inspired Herbert Heath Helman, Philadelphia, to write a poem which was published in The Evening Herald, July 7, 1894.   A copy of this poem is printed in its entirety in Appendix I. Today , church bells ring both inside and outside of many Hanover Churches. Handbell and chime choirs have sprouted in both the churches and as part of the music program in many area schools. Handbell choirs contribute regularly to music ministries at St. Matthew Lutheran Church, Emmanuel United Church of Christ, Lohr's Memorial United Methodist Church, St. Mark Lutheran Church, and Trinty United Church of Christ.

The early craftsmen in Hanover included blacksmiths, shoemakers, tinsmiths, coach makers, coverlet and carpet weavers, iron molders, clock makers, and an organ and harpsichord builder, Adam Ault. Ault owned a two-story brick house, having two rooms and a hall, fronting onto York Street. His dwelling also included a frame one-story kitchen. In the 1830's Mr. Ault used a part of the upper story of the house as a shop where he built church pipe organs and harpsichords. He is credited with building at least twenty organs for churches in the Hanover and northern Maryland region.   He also made gun stocks and shoe lasts. His life and work will be discussed in greater detail later in this book.

Eighty years later another music lover constructed fine violins in his home. Emanuel Meckley, 281 Third St., spent his days as a woodworker in a local factory. He spent his evenings at home making violins using a hammer and chisel to hew the cases from solid locks of hardwood. His early models were fashioned after the Steiner instruments; his later versions were made over the lines of the famous Stradivarius. Today there are two Master Violin Makers in the area; Edward C. Campbell, Boiling Springs, and David M. Waltersdorff, New Oxford.

The earliest musical presentation for which a copy of the printed program has survived, outside of a church dedication service, details a "concert of sacred music by the Lutheran choir" of Hanover dated 1839. The program was found among the personal effects of Philip Thomas and was brought to public notice by George Whims. On June 18, 1912, The <u>Record Herald</u> reprinted the program, originally printed by Joseph Gitt of Hanover, as part of an article featuring Mrs. Abner Forney who was ninety-two years old at the time.. The program details both morning and evening services that day. The address for the morning service was "On the Science of Music " while the evening service's sermon was "On the Subject of Music".

1 George R. Powell. <u>History of York County, Pennsylvania</u>. (Chicago, 1907), pp. 128-129.
2 <u>Ibid.</u>

Early Music Clubs and Societies

The program embraced instrumental and
vocal music of a high order and every
number was rendered with a spirit and
beauty of expression to be expected of the
skillful musicians who form the club.
Review of the Annual Concert of the
Concordia Club
Evening Herald
May 1902

Beyond the church doors, musical clubs and societies
mastered the secular music of the day and perpetuated the
Classics. A Concert Hall was built in the southwest angle of
the Center Square in 1860 by Dr. Vincent E.S. Eckert. The
Hall was part of an Armory built for the Hanover Infantry.
It was Hanover's sole amusement resort for several decades.

The Earliest Clubs and Societies

Hanover's first production company was the Dramatic
Society which organized in December 1822. The group met
twice a week for rehearsals. Their first performance, "The
Merchant of Venice", was staged in a room at Peter Eckerts.
The proceeds collected from performances, usually $12 -
$16 , were always given to the poor. Although not musical
productions, the Society's regularly scheduled rehearsals,
annual productions, and beneficent spirit established a
pattern for later groups to follow.

The Hanover Dramatic and Musical Association was
organized by a group of young people in the 1870's . Some

of its members formed one of Hanover's earliest orchestras. This orchestra performed concerts in the Old Concert Hall. Some of the orchestra members were Prof. Jacob Gundrum, leader; Harry Dietz, violin; Harry Spangler, guitar; Louis Bargett, and William and Hezekiah Heuser. Another fraction of this group split off to form the Amateur Musical Association in 1877

Townsfolk opened their homes to music club meetings and organized performances. The following is a review of the comic opera "Pinafore" that was performed on April 2, 1880 under the direction of Miss Sally Winebrenner. The performance was given at the home of Mrs. Mattie Barnitz whose residence was on Carlisle Street. A select audience of 100 guests attended.

The entertainment took place in one of the spacious parlors which was fitted up for the stage, and promptly at eight o'clock the curtain rose, disclosing the opening scene, the miniature performers all being in proper costume.

The acting and singing throughout the entire play was of such an artistic character as would have done full credit to veteran professionals and some of the youthful performers displaying a remarkable degree of dramatic and vocal talent in their respective parts...

The entertainment was one of the most enjoyable of the kind ever before attempted in our town and afforded

much pleasure and gratification to the
audience.

The following was the cast of characters:

Ralph Rackstraw............ Helen Winebrenner
Boatswain...................... Alfred George
Dick Deadeye................. Harry Schriver
Sir Joseph Porter...K.C.B... Carrie George
Captain Corcoran.............. Codie Young
Josephine.......................... Emma Barnitz
Buttercup........................... Kate Winebrenner
Hebe................................ Mabel Trone
Sisters- Cousins - Aunts: Minnie Grove, Annie
Forney, Nettie Forney, George Bittinger, and 3 year
old Aimee Wirt
Sailors............................. Eddy Winebrenner and
Bob Hamme

The Haydn Oratorio Society

Hanover's earliest formally organized musical society was
the Haydn Oratorio Society formed in May 1885. The
nucleus for the club were the members of an oratorio class
that met three-quarters of the year under the instruction of
Prof. George H. Lane. He was the organist and choirmaster
of Grace Protestant Episcopal Church in Baltimore and was
elected the group's choral director.

Officers elected at the organizational meeting were:
Rev. George Scholl, D.D., Pres.; Rev. J. C. Bowman, Vice-
Pres.; A. M. Schmidt, Sec. ; George A. Long, Treas. ; and
Miss Lucy Forney, Organist. It was hoped that the Oratorio
Society would serve as a seedbed to train choir members for
the local churches. Hence, the group always nurtured
strong ties to local churches and involved the clergy in

promoting its efforts. The balance of the first Board of Managers included: Miss Martha Dellone, Mrs. Charles E. Etzler, Mrs. R.M. Wirt, Mrs. George R Powell, Misses Ida Young, Alice Hilbish, and M. Joe Wolff.

In November of 1885, the Haydn Oratorio Society gave their first concert in the Concert Hall. The Hanover Herald gave the concert a dubious review stating:

> The solo and duets were all well sung, while the quartette, the only glimpse of humor in the entertainment, was well received...

> The concert, however was not what might be called a 'popular' one, and we suggest to the Society, that at future concerts, the program be so arranged as to contribute also to the entertainment of the large portion of the public not yet educated up to the appreciation of the beauties of classical music.

Over the next decade Hanoverians' musical tastes leaped up on the classical music appreciation curve. The coverage afforded the Haydn Oratorio Society's sacred musical concert held on December 12, 1894, could well be mistaken for a review of a concert by today's Hanover Community Singers. Portions of the review in the Evening Herald read:

> The musical event of the season was the presentation in St. Matthew's Lutheran Church last night of Gaul's Sacred Cantata "The Holy City" by the Haydn Oratorio Society of Hanover ably assisted by Mrs. W. E. Parson of Washington, D.C., and Miss Leila Snyder of Baltimore.

The event was long anticipated by our
people and the large church was completely
filled with the best citizens of the town,
(most of whom had relatives or friends
among the singers)... The concert was under
the direction of Prof. Frederick W. Wolff...
the instructor of the Oratorio Society. The
performance in every sense was a successful
one and showed in a gratifying manner the
ability of our vocal singers.

The Beethoven Club

Hanover's longest -lived, formally organized musical
society was its Beethoven Club. The Beethoven Club of
Hanover was founded in 1892 at the home of Miss Charlotte
Hauser, 317 Baltimore St. Charter members of the
organization were Miss M.W. Hauser, Mr. and Mrs. J.D.
Zouck, Miss Emily J. Young, Mr. And Mrs. C.W. Corbin,
Miss Charlotte and Anna Hauser, Mrs. Guy Newcomer,
Miss Miriam Welsh, and Dr. M.M. Fleagle. Miss Young
served as the club's first president and assumed all
responsibility for the programs.

By 1900, club membership had grown to twenty-six
members and entertainment for the group's monthly
meetings was provided by students from Charlotte Hauser's
music class. As membership increased to seventy-eight
members, the programs were expanded to include selections
by the local Glee Club and by a small orchestra composed of
Dr. M. .M. Fleagle, H.E. Hoke, Dr. C.P. Wolcott, Paul
Zeiber, and George Zouck.

Prompted by a proposal from printer-historian, William
Anthony, the Beethoven Club of Hanover sponsored the
John Luther Long Birthplace Memorial Tablet Committee

Plaque, John Luther Long birthplace, 43, Frederick Street,
razed 1980 (approx.).Photo courtesy of the Hanover Public
Library.

on February 16, 1948. It was Long who had written the story "Madame Butterfly" which served as the basis for the libretto of Puccini's famous opera by the same name. Under the signature of Elizabeth Howells, Secretary-Treasurer of the Memorial Tablet Committee, contributions were solicited from the community to help pay for the expenses of the tablet and the broadcasting of the dedication services.

The tablet, erected by the Beethoven Club of Hanover on the Long Homestead on April 4, 1948, cited John Luther Long as a distinguished son of Hanover, PA. He was a lawyer, playwright, and novelist. The community erected the tablet in acknowledgment of the honor he brought to his native town. The Long homestead was razed in the 1980's. In 1991 the Hanover Garden Club had a new plaque cast and re-dedicated recognizing Long's achievements.

The Concordia Club

The Concordia Club formed six years after the Beethoven Club and started out pursing a duel program; one that included both performance and education. While special concerts and elaborate social events accentuate this group's history, an annual music education program was also an important part of their organization. This was noted in the following excerpt from a feature in the Evening Herald printed on June 4, 1901.

> The Concordia Club is composed of Hanover's most talented lovers of music. The meetings during the winter were held every two weeks, a course of study being prepared by a committee, which this year was the Wagnerian Opera.

Much of interest and value pertaining to
music and musicians was discussed at these
meeting. The members were thus kept well-
informed on all events in the realm of music.

The Club's membership list reads like a "Who's Who" list
in Hanover's musical community at that time. Some of
those included were: J. Frank Frysinger, Nellie and Edna
Powell, R.L. Erhart and wife, Mrs. M. D. Bishop, Mrs. W.
R. Soliday, Grace Zieber, Elizabeth Fitz, Mary Cook, Cora
Colehouse, Anna Hauser, H. C. Naill, Paul Zieber, George
A. Long, Jules Spillman, Edward Holmes, Dr. M.M.
Fleagle, and R. L. Hamme.

Concordia Club meetings were held in private homes so
guests at the meeting were limited to two per member. An
invitation card was required for admittance to any of their
meetings or concerts.

Members gave an annual concert for the pleasure of their
friends and families. The events drew large and fashionable
crowds of about 400 guests by invitation only. They were
billed as the social event of the year. In May of 1902 their
annual concert was held in the Opera House. The Evening
Herald carried the event as its lead story. A partial
description follows.

The stage presented a brilliant spectacle,
having never before, perhaps, as beautifully and
as tastefully decorated. The lights were turned
low and the illumination of a wood scene was
by Chinese lanterns suspended from above.
Palms and plants were arranged with taste and
easy chairs and rockers furnished the seats for
the performers. At the rear was a small
fountain...

The Hanover Concert Association

Hanover's musical heritage is peppered with organizations formed to promote a variety of musical offerings to the community. In 1934 the Hanover Concert Association formed as a sponsor for the Hanover Civic Orchestra. Mrs. W. Frank Cox, Jr., served as president and Luther H. Redclay served as secretary -treasurer. Members were entitled to seats for two concerts that year.

By 1940 the Hanover Concert Association ticket package offered holders six attractions including three concerts by the Civic Orchestra. Membership fees, which included tickets to all the Concert Association sponsored events were $3.00 for adults and $1.50 for students. As an additional inducement for that season, new members were also entitled to attend the Hanover Civic Orchestra's Annual Spring Concert featuring harpist Rebecca Lewis.

The St. Matthew's Concert Series

Since 1981 Hanoverians have been treated to performances by world renown artists as well as local talent through the St. Matthew's Concert Series held annually at St. Matthew's Lutheran Church, Chestnut St., Hanover. Administered by the church's Minister of Music, Scott G. Fredericks, this series has featured such artists as organists Diane Bish, Simon Preston, and James Dale. World-traveled choirs such as the American Boys Choir and the Cathedral Choir of England have performed in the chancel. The bi-annual concerts performed by the 180- voice choir, The Hanover Community Singers, are a community favorite in this series.. Admission is free to the public for all these concerts. The St. Matthew Concert Series is solely supported through benefactors, patrons, and public contributions.

And the Bands Played

Band music is the commonest expression
of the instrumental music of a community.
Recognized as such at most other places, it
was always considered such in this place ,
with the result that our people were always
ready to lend their support in greater or
lessor manner to such organizations. The
reputation of the local bands rendered at the
time of their existence was always very
complimentary to their ability...

The Record Herald
May 8, 1925

While there is enough material available on the bands of
Hanover to fill a separate volume, for the purposes of this
publication, only a select sampling will be detailed . Also,
while there were well-known bands in Brodbecks and
McSherrystown, for our purposes, the bands presented here
will be exclusively from Hanover. Some of the most
recognizable bands in Hanover's history include: Hanover's
Patriotic Order of the Sons of America Band, The Union
Band, the Harmonica Silver Cornet Band, the Hanover City
Band, The Cresent Band, the Knights of Pythias Band, the
Lyric Band, the Hanover Legion and VFW Drum and Bugle
Corps, Pratt's School of Music String Band, the Hanover
Oahu String Band, and the Hanover High School and Junior
High Bands. The list of bands is so extensive that a
chronological listing has been made in Appendix II.

Some of the dates and names may vary slightly as it seemed to be a common practice to organize a band, play together for several years, and then merge with another existing band or just form a new band with the same members under a different name. This list only includes public, school, and club bands. Many private or specialized bands such as the Gobrechts' Little German Band also entertained at festivals, family reunions, county fairs, and banquets.

The Earliest Bands

As previously noted , Hanover's earliest bands were drum corps and martial bands organized to serve in the Revolutionary War and the War of 1812. Brass bands did not appear in the area until the 1840's when the tuba, bugle , and cornet-a-piston were introduced into band instrumentation.

The earliest organized brass band in the area was the Union Band. According to newspaper articles dated in the 1890's , this band was formed somewhere between 1840 and 1842 under the leadership of William Bange. Prof. William Young, a noted bugler, was the instrumental instructor. Young later served a bugler in the 11th Pennsylvania Calvary during the Civil War. This group disbanded with the outbreak of the Mexican War in 1846.

In Gibson's History of York County , the name Union Band surfaces, perhaps as re-organized and not as a new band, in 1852 through the efforts of Capt. D.Q. Albright. An article in a 1897 isssue of The Evening Herald credits Albright with organizing the Hanover Brass Band in 1857. Here the discrepancies in names and dates end since both articles expound on the excellence of these early bands. This early band was familiarly known as the "Silver Band" because of their magnificent Tyrolese silver instruments which were imported from Vienna, Austria at the cost of $1000. An E-flat cornet, played by H. Clay Metger, cost $100.

The sax section of this band formed a side group known as the Silver Sax Horn Band. They sometimes played at wedding receptions, reunions, or other small gatherings. On occassion, they took it upon themselves to serenade private citizens as a special recognition. One such incident was reported on the front page of the Hanover Spectator, September 9, 1859. It reads, " On Wednesday evening the members of the Silver Sax Horn Band proceded with their instruments to the residence of G.W.Welsh, Esq. and paid him the handsome compliment of a serenade in honor of his nomination." Welsh had been nominated as a candidate for the next State Legislature.

The elegant wagon used by the Hanover Brass Band cost $500. In 1863 this group disbanded as many of its member entered military service.

The Civil War dissipated the town's band ranks until 1868 when the Hanover Silver Cornet Band organized. This band merged with the local orchestra known as "Free and Easy" in 1886 to form the City Band. For all its ability, this band seems to have constantly suffered a shortage of operating funds. The Evening Herald, July 9, 1902, ran a front page article calling for liberal subscriptions from the locals to keep the band up to standards. This feature gives some hints of the needs and costs of maintaining a community band at the turn of the twentieth century. A portion of this article reads:

> It is merely a question of support
> that will decide the continuation of the
> open-air concerts. In some instances,

This photo of the Hanover Silver Cornet Band was taken
circa 1898. Front row; third from left, Riley Humbert; fifth,
Henry McKinney ; sixth, Spencer Hoffman ; seventh from
left Willard Heusner . Second row, Lewis Kluck; fifth,
Edward Moul ; sixth, John Zinn. Third Row, George Zinn ;
second, Louis D. Sell; third, George Schmidt; fourth,
Charles Bowman ; fifth, Lewis Bargelt ; At extreme right,
director Clark S. McKallip; others in photography
unidentified. Photo courtesy of Hanover Public Library.

some individuals have not favored the
cause at all applying the term
begging...

There are men of means in Hanover
who could give $100 each a year and
not be embarrassed. Every man,
woman, boy and girl can afford to give
25 or 50 cents a year for the public
benefit.

The band needs new equipment
throughout. They need a new band
stand erected at a point of easy access
to all. And, they need a regular fund
of not less that $500 a year to
successfully carry on business.

In addition to asking for subscriptions, the band also
raised money by having its director give music lessons .
Here, membership in the band carried financial benefits. If
a pupil planned to join the band or an orchestra when they
became proficient on their instrument, they were charged 25
cents per hour for their lesson. If no such commitment was
anticipated, they were charged 50 cents per hour. None of
these efforts appear to have been successful since references
to the City Band disappear from the literature around 1903.

As a note of interest, the dis-banding of the City Band
unwittingly provided the Gobrecht brothers with their first
brass instrument. Clifford Gobrecht purchased a
cornet from a former band member and practiced at the
home of his uncle Calvin Unger with whom he lived.
Because he wanted to quickly become musically proficient
on his newly acquired horn, he practiced day and night and
in all areas of the house. The rest of the family was not

impressed and issued Clifford an ultimatum, give up playing the cornet or move out. Clifford gave the trumpet to another nephew who lived close by, Levi J. Gobrecht, and that got the ball rolling in the musical field at John A. Gobrecht's house.

The Knights of Pythias Band

As the sun set on the history of the Hanover City Band, a new star was rising for one of Hanover's best known and longest -lived bands. The 16 member nucleus of the Hanover Knights of Pythias Band Lodge No. 318 first met in October 1903. The first officers were C. Edward Bowman, president, Louis Hankle, secretary, H. K. Billet, treasurer, and William E. Frock, conductor. Throughout its early years this band was supported by the Lodge which helped the band stave off the financial deficiencies that had plagued the City Band.

The first rehearsal was held on the porch of C. Edward Bowman's home of Fair Avenue. The Hanover group merged with Company 7 in Lancaster, U.R. K. Of P., in 1904 for a combined total of 21 members.

In 1910 Brigadier J. M. Reichard officially named the group the Second Regimen Pennsylvania Brigade Band. It was then the largest K. Of P. Band in the United States with 57 members. The band played performances in Cleveland, Sea City, Pittsburgh, Boston, Baltimore, Altoona, and Oil City. The band's reputation was built on its varied repertoire which included not only march classics, but also works by Rossini, Sibelius, Schubert, and Beethoven.

Edward J. Gobrecht took on the directorship of the band in the early 1930's and demanded professionalism and commitment from his players. As a result, their concert were

The Uniform Rank, Knights of Pythias pose in front of the
Hanover Saving Fund Society Building, 1914.

of the finest quality and played to capacity crowds. For example, their 1935 Annual Spring Concert featured Dr. Frank Simon as soloist and guest conductor. Simon was billed as "America's Foremost Cornetist" at the time.

The Moose Band

The K of P Band had its home with the parent lodge, No. 318, until 1956 when because of declining membership, the lodge moved from the Shepperd Building on Carlisle Street to Blouse's Furniture Center on Baltimore Street. The facilities there were inadequate for band practice forcing them to look for new headquarters. They accepted an invitiation from Hanover Lodge 227, Loyal Order of Moose, to make their new home there. The organization then changed its name from U.R.K. of P. Band to the Moose Band of Hanover.

This new Moose Band, still under the direction of Edward J. Gobrecht, made its first public appearance in a concert of popular music on June 4, 1956 in Wirt Park as a feature of Hanover Heritage Days. For years to come, the Moose Band would be perennial favorites in parades, at picnics and socials, and at community concerts. The band promoted the activities of the Moose Lodge just as they had at the Lodge of the Knights of Pythias. They even had their own song.

The Moose Song
(March 1960)

Join the Moose Lodge you'll find they're
grand,
It's the best Lodge in the land.
With love and charity as their motto,
They work hand in hand.

Hanover Lodge #227 Moose Band. First row (bottom):
Paul Stauffer, Edward Warner, Ray Markle, Burnell Wentz,
Louis Reifsnider, Clarence Blocker, Jr., Herman Wentz,
Ron Birgensmith, Robert Rittace, Gordon Zartman. Second
row: Ronald Wentz, William Reese, David Yingling,
Clarence Myers, Joseph Gobrecht, Earl Leppo, Ronal
Bollinger, Ralph Myers, Ray Wilson, Emory Gobrecht.
Third row: Edgar Wisensale, Larry Blocker, William Spar,
Samuel Huggens, Thomas Noel, Wayne Helwig, Thomas
Zimmerman, Donald Tasto, Homer Fuhrman, Nevin
Raubenstine. Fourth row: Gilbert Allewelt, William
Gobrecht, Gerald Wentz, Donald Sterner, Ned Shaffer,
Edward J. Gobrecht, Sr., Director.

They care for members right from the start
They care for children at Mooseheart.
With a place for old folks at Moosehaven
They always do their part.

We're the Moose Band
And we'll play for you.
And our very best we'll try to do.
We'll sing and play the styles of music
That keep you from feeling blue.

The Lyric Band

The Lyric Band of Hanover strikes a chord of recognition
with residence in both the Hanover area and northern
Maryland. The band was founded on November 1, 1932 in
the Parkville Fire Company Hall. There were 36 musicians
present at the organizational meeting. Its earliest rehearsals,
under the directorship of H. W . Swartzbaugh, were held in
the engine house of the fire company.

In 1933, the band moved to the former Melhorn building.
In 1938 the band purchased the old YMCA building,
complete with swimming pool, at 20 York Street. This
building is still the band's headquarters. The band made its
first public appearance in Hanover's 1933 Memorial Day
Parade.

The band was incorporated on a non-profit basis in May
1939. For a time, the Lyric Band also maintained a Junior
Band and ran a nightclub with dancing in the hall. It has
always been non-sectarian and independent of affliations
with any lodge or society. Its membership is open to all
skilled local band musicians. Its players are all members of
the American Federation of Musicians Local #49.

Member of the Lyric Band of Hanover pose prior to one of
their concerts in the Park Theater. Photo courtesy Poist
Studio, Hanover, PA.

Today, the band performs in parades and offers a summer concert series at the Band Shell in Codorus State Park on Sunday evenings. In adddition to the concert band, there is also a stage band and a "Good Times" Jazz Band.

The American Legion Post 14 Drum and Bugle Corps- Today's Lancers

The oldest instrumental organization in Hanover today is the Hanover Lancers Senior Drum and Bugle Corps American Legion Post 14. This group grew out of the seedstock of the Harold H. Bair American Legion Post 14 Drum and Bugle Corps founded in 1920. The date appears in some publications as 1922, but 1920 is currently the accepted date. The group celebrated its 75 th Anniversary in 1995, publishing a special Seventy-Fifth Anniversry Commerative Yearbook.

The Harold H. Bair American Legion Post 14 was organized by returning World War I veterans and received its charter in August, 1920. Edwin Kline was elected the Post's first Commander. Kline had marched with the U S Marine Corps Band as a bass drum player from 1917 to 1919. Commander Kline and the approxiamtely 100 members of the new Legion decided to form a musical unit to march with veterans in parades and celebrations. Thus, the Harold H. Bair American Legion Post 14 Drum and Bugle Corps was born.

At the time, the post occupied " The Hole" beneath the York Railways Terminal Station. The post assisted the corps financially at the start by purchasing a dozen bugles, four snare drums, and a bass drum. Total costs of the instruments was $147.00 .

The Harold H. Bair American Legion Post 14 Drum and Bugle Corps. This photo was taken at the Hanover Savings Fund Society Building, now the Bank of Hanover, at 25 Carlisle Street on May 29, 1928. Photo courtesy of Nancy Leister.

The corps practiced in the terminal basement until Post 14 moved into the Carlisle Street building. The Drum Corp also then moved into an old structure on Park Avenue at the rear of the Legion Home. On cold nights, the members kept a fire in the old stove, taking turns supplying fuel. They practiced nightly, their music staffs illuminated by tallow drips or ancient lamps and lanterns.

Originally, the members marched in the uniforms they were discharged in; Army, Navy, and Marine Corps. In 1921, new uniforms were purchased for all corp members. They wore white shirts with black ties, white duck pants, and Legion "overseas" caps. In the past seventy-five years, the group has had fourteen different uniforms. Ed "Diddles" Kline was the corps Drum Major and Director.

Drum Corps activity continued to grow mainly in the eastern and mid-western states in the 1930's and '40's. By the mid 1930's, the Hanover Corp had polished themselves into a crack musical, marching unit. In 1934, they marched in the Shenandoah Apple Blossom Festival Parade, winning the Grand Prize of $300 and a $150 scholarship, which they awarded to an Eichelberger High student. In ensuing years, they would go on to win six more firsts, one second, and one third place in the Apple Blossom parades.

The corps, like most other community musical groups, weathered triumphs and tragedies. In 1948, a fire swept through the Legion Home destroying $15,000 worth of the the corps' uniforms and instruments. The corps re-built and have continued to change with the times. In 1958 they followed a trend set by other corps and changed their name to reflect the insigna on their uniforms. By the margin of one vote, they changed their name to the Hanover Lancers Drum and Bugle Corps .

One thing that has remained unchanged is the loyalty and commaradie members derive from participating in drum corp competition. In their Seventy-Fifth Commerative Yearbook, Randy Kemp tries to explain this attachment by posing this question. " Did you ever try to explain to someone who doesn't know Drum Corps why you would practice three nights a week, get on a bus Friday night, practice all day Saturday to perform a ten minute show wearing a funny looking suit and hat... not get paid for it, in fact spend money to do it, and can't wait to do it again next week? "

And the Orchestras Played

The High School Orchestra, under the leadership of Mr. Gantt, furnished music for our exercises at Chapel and provided snappy tunes to help the eager (?) students up the stairs and to various classes. Spillman's playing was marvelous. "Dutch" set the time and took the lead and the others followed if they could. Spangler's cornet ran a close second and Miss Bair's handling of the unwieldy trombone proved her skill. At times Stover added to the harmony with a banjo-mandolin, and the second violin part was carried by Crawford. On the whole they provided an impetus that was felt in all recitation rooms , and blue were the days they failed to appear.

The Nornir 1921

Hanover's town orchestras have come in all sizes and affiliations. Piecing together the jigsaw picture of Hanover's early orchestras is difficult since the townsfolk often called anything short of a full brass band, an orchestra. Today we would have called many of the town's earliest orchestras ensembles or chamber orchestras . An ensemble is a small group of supporting musicians playing music in two or more parts. Orchestras usually have multiple sections such as strings, brass, woodwinds, and percussion with several players in each section. An example of what people called an orchestra in Hanover in the 1890's was a group known as Egger's Orchestra. With Edward Egger as its Musical Director, the orchestra was comprised of a flute, a violin, a clarinet, cornet, piano, trombone, and double bass.

The Earliest Orchestras

Many of Hanover's earliest orchestras were also auxiliary units of existing bands, with a handful of select musicians playing in both groups. Often these orchestras would melt away or just fold into an existing band. A chronology of Hanover's orchestras can be found in Appendix III.

The earliest mention of a town orchestra in the local papers appears around 1859. It was organized by a violinist, Prof. James Hoffman, who also served as its musical director. In the winter of 1859 and early 1860, this orchestra joined with a comedy troupe and performed dramatic and minstrel shows in York, Adams, Franklin Counties, and throughout northern Maryland. Due to the lack of funding, they played for only one season. The group disbanded in the spring of 1860 with Prof. Hoffman heading off to Baltimore.

A German immigrant, Prof. Jacob Gundrum , was to have a long and fortuitous impact on Hanover's musical community. As mentioned earlier, it was Prof. Gundrum who organized Hanover's Silver Cornet Band in 1868 which was so admired in its day. The tentacles of Gundrum's musical talents and enthusiasm reached into numerous musical groups and societies. Gundrum recognized that re-establishing a town band and an orchestra on the heels of the Civil War would provide the town with both entertainment and signal the return of pre-war community activities.

In 1866 Gundrum organized an orchestra know as "Free and Easy". Its music was in constant demand for picnics,

The Lutheran Church Orchestra 1898 preparing for an outdoor concert. Left to right: Robert Ehrhart, Lorin A. Rohrbaugh, Josiah S. Moul, Hezekiah Heusner, Millar Heusner, Edward H. Moul, Harry D. Ehrhart, __ ------- Krug, George A. Long. Seated at the organ, Prof. Jacob A. Gundrum. Seated: Mrs. Dan Ehrhart, Miss M. Joe Wolf (later Mrs. Ehrhart), Mrs. George Long, and Miss Trone (later Mrs. J. J. Bair). Photo courtesy of the Hanover Public Library.

parties, and weddings. But, like earlier orchestras, it existed on its own for only about six years and then merged back into the Hanover Silver Cornet Band.

Another small orchestra was formed in 1870 by members of Hanover's Dramatic and Musical Society. A group of less than 10 players, they often performed in the Old Concert Hall and accompanied the dramatic productions staged by the Society. Prof. Jacob Gundrum is also listed as the leader of this group.

The Sunday School Orchestras

While efforts were made to keep orchestral groups flourishing in Hanover, as evidenced by the formation of the Philharmonic Society in 1899, they seemed to have fallen out of favor until around 1910 when orchestras were embraced by the local Sunday School programs.

St. Paul's Evangelical Lutheran Church on York Street organized its Sunday School Orchestra in 1910 with Chester Leese as director. The St. Paul's Orchestra played regularly for the adult Sunday School Services and for special occassions in church. In 1933, it played the Lutheran Reunion at Pen-Mar . Harry Swartzbaugh directed the orchestra from 1914 until 1925 when he was succeeded by Edward J. Goebrecht. The surname Gobrecht has become synonymous with music in Hanover ever since that time.

Emory A. Gobrecht credits the six Gobrecht brothers' involvement in Sunday School Orchestras as the impetus for their musical success as a family. In his Home Spun Philosopy Book 2, page 2 he writes:

It is my opinion that Trinity Church should
be credited with the musical success of the
Goebrecht family. Upon signing of the
Armistice terminating World War I, I was
discharged from the Army and returned to
my home in Hanover. It was then I began
playing in the Sunday School Orchestra at
Trinity Church. At that time Miss Lella
Rudisill was the organist and also was in
charge of the Sunday School Orchestra. In
1920 I was appointed the orchestra leader...
This appointment served as an incentive and
shortly after my Sunday School appointment,
I conceived the idea of the six Goebrecht
Brothers forming a band.

The Six Gobrecht Bros. Orchestra

The Six Gobrecht Bros. Orchestra was comprised of Levi
playing cornet and drums, William playing the bass, Clayton
the piano, and Edward a cornet, trombone, and violin.
Joseph, who could play any bass horn, was assigned the
saxophone, and Emory played the xylophone. With the
support of a Consistory member A.R. Brodbeck, the brothers
obtained approval from Rev. Roth to use Trinity's Sunday
School Auditorium for the premier concert of their new
orchestra. The rental charge for the use of the auditorium
was set at $10 to cover the electric light expenses. Over 300
people attented that first concert with a collection totally
approximatedly $400. The church waived its electric light
charges.

After their first concert, the brothers were recruited by
several other local churches to either come start a Sunday
School Orchestra at that church or to come take charge of an
existing one. As a result, Edward took charge of the St.

Paul's Sunday School Orchestra, as previously mentioned. Emory helped initiate orchestras at Dub's Church and at a church in Spring Grove.

The Hanover High School Orchestra

Hanover High School organized the earlist high school orchestra in the area. Pictured in the inaugural issue of the Nornir in 1921, the orchestra was composed of Edna Senft, leader; Paul Spillman, first violin ; Myrl Crawford, second violin ; LeRoy Nace, saxophone; Richard Stover, mandolin bange ; Roger Fleagle, flute ; Eugene Spangler, Ira Melhorn and Elwood Hamm, Cornets ; Carroll Mehring and Diller Wierman, clarinets ; Bernice Bair, trombone ; and Ruth Melhorn, piano. Their advisor was Mr. Gantt, the French teacher.

The Royal Club Orchestra

The Club Royal Orchestra had its beginnings as a High School group in 1928, playing at dances. The group played for all types of dances and performed in the summers at Williams Grove Park. The Apple Blossom Festival, held annually in Winchester, VA, was a regular stand for the group.

In its early days, the group was fronted by Peabody Conservatory of Music graduate Guy Luchenbaugh, an excellent teacher and violinist. Later, the orchestra was directed by Jack Shaller. Richard Feezer, a member of the original orchestra and trumpet player, wielded the baton after Shaller and until the group disbanded in 1942. Members of the Club Royal Orchestra were: piano, "Chappy" Dell; string bass, Jack Hopkens; drums, Dick Rebert; guitar, Sidney Smith; vibes/guitar Marlan Shearer; saxaphone, John Spangler, Fred Bosseman, Ernie Hossler, and Leroy

Hoffheins; trumpet, Richard Feezer, Dick Markle, and Charles Geesey ; and trombone, George Little.

The Hanover Civic Orchestra

Dr. M.M. Fleagle, an outstanding physical and talented violinist, devoted much of his spare time in his later years to organizing and directing local instrumental groups. One such group was Fleagle's Parlor Orchestra. It consisted of 24 pieces with Dr. Fleagle as conductor. This group was in such demand to perform for various occasions, that it quickly became evident that a civic orchestra was needed. In 1932 the Parlor Orchestra evolved into the Hanover Civic Orchestra. Dr. Fleagle served as its first conductor with Walter Schultz as concertmeister.

The 57 piece orchestra performed its first public concert in the Park Theater on Wednesday evening, June 22, 1932. Mrs. Viola Brodbeck Fleagle, a coloratura soprano and the conductor's wife, was the guest artist. Featured as soloists or in solo parts were: Emory Gobrecht, cornet, Edward Gobrecht, trombone, Oscar Bowman, Flute, and Raymond Zepp, clarinet. Paul A. Harner conducted his own composition, the "President Washington March".

In February 1933 a second concert was given with Mrs. W. Frank Cox, Jr., soprano and Raymond Zepp, clarinet, as soloists. Along with Doris Baker, pianist, those named above would become synonymous with the Hanover Civic Orchestra.

The Hanover Concert Association formed in 1934 with the intent of acting as sponsor for the Hanover Civic Orchestra. The Association promoted ticket sales for the three annual orchestral concerts , sponsored musical trivia contest in the paper, and handled much of the orchestra's publicity. Mrs.

MUSIC CONTEST

SPONSORED BY

Hanover Concert Association

Headquarters: Hotel Richard McAllister
HANOVER, PA.

Here are the questions -- good luck!

1. Who wrote the "Coffee Cantata?"
2. Is the composer of the "Rhapsody in Blue" still alive?
3. Which symphony is known as "Beethoven's Tenth?"
4. Name the American composer who wrote a composition based on the flood disaster of 1937?
5. What famous composer of symphonies wrote one opera? What is that opera called?
6. What famous composer of opera wrote one symphony? What is that symphony called?
7. Who founded the Salzburg Festival?
8. What American Composer played at the World's Fair every day?
9. Who is known as "the Father of Symphony?"
10. What composer wrote music to describe walking in the snow?
11. Three famous musicians were child prodigies. Who are they?
12. Who was Richard Geyer?
13. Name three different operas by three different composers in each one of which one of the male of the male roles is sung by a woman.
14. Who are the three B's in music?
15. What musician today is well known as a composer, conductor and soloist?
16. Who is the most famous American composer of the 19th Century?
17. What State in the United States boasts two outstanding symphony organizations?
18. What is the name of the man who is a leader of a swing band and who also plays classical music with a string quartette?
19. Identify the following: (1) Bartok; (2) DeFalla; (3) Poulene; (4) Barbirolli; (5) Honegger?
20. In what symphony do we find Schiller's "Ode to Joy" incorporated?
21. How many symphonies has Jean Sibelius written?
22. Who wrote "Amelia Goes to the Ball", "The Devil and Daniel Webster" and "The Flying Dutchman?"
23. Identify the following: "Old Maid and the Thief," Serge Kousevitzky, Bayreuth, Fray and Braggiotti, Tito Shipa.
24. Did Mozart and Beethoven ever meet?
25. With what famous composer is the name of Madame Von Meck associated? Did she meet the composer?

1. Contest closes Friday, May 3, at 7 P.M.
2. Bring your answers to Headquarters. Winners will be announced Saturday, May 4.

The Hanover Concert Association founded in 1934 often ran contests such as this one printed in the April 22,1940 issue of the Hanover Evening Sun .

W. Frank Cox, Jr., served as its first president with Luther H. Redclay serving as secretary-treasurer. The advent of WWII demanded many of Hanover's finest for military service and the orchestra dispersed.

The Hanover Symphony

Spawned by the desire of several local musicians to again have an orchestra in which Hanover's best trained instrumentalists could perform, the Hanover Symphony Board organized in 1995 with the intent of forming and promoting the Hanover Symphony. Serving on the first Hanover Symphony Board of Directors were Richard Carson, President, Joseph Clark, Vice-President, Debbie Kuntz, Secretary, Linda Cole, Treasurer, Larry Kuntz, Musical Director, and Susan Gross, Personnel Manager. Completing the first Board were Pat Carey, Nancy Leister, Deborah Dennin, Joyce Elsner, and Gail Rhodes.

On November 5, 1995 the Hanover Symphony Orchestra played its debut concert in the Hanover High School Auditorium under the baton of Larry Kuntz. Since then, the orchestra has made the re-furbished Eichelberger Performing Arts Center its permanent home.

Much of the orchestra's success can be contributed to five persons who originally organized the group during the summer of 1995. They were: Larry Kuntz, conductor; Joe Clark and Susan Gross who recruited member musicians, and Richard Carson and Debra Kuntz who handled the group's finances.

In addition to serving as a performance outlet for many fine musicians who provide their audience with quality performances of fine music, the Hanover Symphony Orchestra has established a scholarship program to promote continuing education for its musicians. The Symphony Board grants six personal scholarships and one school district appreciation award annually. The school district appreciation award is granted on a rotating basis to Hanover, Delone, South Western, Spring Grove, New Oxford, and Littlestown districts to support music education and performance. Two personal scholarships of $2000 each and four scholarships of $300 each are awarded within the orchestra's membership at their spring concert.

Choirs and Choruses

The General Committee of the
Centennial visited the Eichelberger School
building to listen to the Community Choir.
With them was a stranger. The impression
made upon the stranger follows in his own
words:
..."As I left the hall where those men and
women sang, their songs followed me... and
I felt proud that I had the honor to be
associated in even the humblest way with a
people who could enter into the spirit of an
occasion with such fine accord. And as I
continued on my way I knew only one
regret: that I could not claim as my own
home town the little city which shelters the
spirit which voices its love of home and
expresses its hospitality in song ..."

The Evening Sun
September 10, 1915

Hanover has had an on-again, off-again love affair with its
choirs and community choruses. In early Hanover the
singing in the choirs struck such a note of discord that it
prompted this editorial to the Hanover Guardian, March 13,
1828. It calls for the improvement of the singing at Sunday
services by hiring a professional music teacher to train the
children to sing. Its author is unknown. It reads:

It must be evident to all persons attending
public worship in the churches of his place,
that such part of the service appertaining to
Sacred song, might be considerably

improved. Notably improved. With
certainty we can say, if not attended to
before long, the remnant of that Choir which
now on some occasions so thinly appears in
the galleries, will still be liable to a farther
diminution from the effect of 'time and tides
changes'...

We consider the present an auspicious
moment for forming a Singing School: and at
the request of some of our neighbors would
wish to direct the attention of our citizens to
this important subject. The "Hanover
Sunday School' contains many children of
both sexes, who gifted by nature with fine
voices, would furnish a sufficient number of
pupils for the formation of a Choir, and
whose talents only require cultivation to
make them good singers...

It is hoped, that we have a sufficient
number of well disposed citizens and heads
of families in this place, who will contribute
so liberally as to enable the officers to
employ an instructor in music and procure
the necessary books for this desirable
purpose.

While the community trained its children to sing, adult
vocalists performed mostly as soloists in small groups in
churches or as part of the occasional school programs at the
Hanover Academy. However, vocalists of all ages were an
integral part of the "Old Folks" Concerts that were give in
the Old Concert Hall in the mid-1870's. These concerts
were organized as amateur talent shows. Their programs
were filled with singing, dramatic readings, and tableaus.

These concerts usually raised about $100, with the proceeds being donated to a charitable cause.

The Haydn Oratorio Society

The Haydn Oratorio Society, formed in 1885, was Hanover's first organized community chorus. The Society had a close relationship with the churches. It was hoped that the vocal training the Society's adult members received under the director Prof. F. W. Wolff, would help improve the choirs in their churches. Eventually the Haydn Oratorio Society's concerts became community favorites, yet support for a community chorus again waned and the Society disbanded around 1896.

The Hanover Oratorio Society

In January 1901, local music enthusiasts called for the organization of the Hanover Oratorio Society. The neighboring town of York, which was the county seat, had a very prominent Oratorio Society at this time. Interest in music or musical training was not a pre-requisite to membership as detailed in the front-page article featured in the Evening Herald, January 4, 1901. It urged,

> It is hoped that this movement will receive the encouragement it merits. If you are interested in music, join the society and become more so, if possible. If you are not, connect yourself with this society and you will surely become interested...If you have a trained voice, join them. If your voice is not trained, join them and it will become trained.

The Hanover Oratorio Society in front of the Hanover
Opera House. Photo courtesy of the Hanover Public
Library

Fourteen months later the group made its debut performance with its rendition of Gaul's historic cantata, "Joan of Arc", under the direction of Prof. W.H. Newborough. The front-page review in the <u>Evening Herald</u> was complimentary to the Oratorio Society but admonished the size of the audience stating,

> The whole rendition was in every way a great credit to the society , and especially Prof. Newborough, who was zealous and untiring in the rehearsals and last evening inspired each singer to put forth his or her best efforts.

> It is regretted that the house (the Opera House) was not crowded to the doors, for the society deserved greater encouragement for their very successful work and their efforts to raise the musical standard in Hanover.

The Hanover High Glee Club

The Hanover Oratorio Society faded from the new chronicles, but a love for contemporary choral music mushroomed in its place. The Hanover High School Glee Club performed not only in schools concerts, but was in demand at Lodge Meetings and company picnics. The 1921 Nornir speaks of the Glee Club,

> "...Never before had the Hanover High heard such a chorus Their selections were most ably rendered and afford much pleasure to the student body. 'Polly' Pitts, perhaps the only one of us possessing real vocal talent, delighted all present by her singing on many

occasions. We expect to hear someday that
she has become famous. The Male Chorus'
rendition of 'The Bull Dog' on one occasion
showed their skill as vocalists and was
greatly appreciated. The solos of Margaret
Morning and Margaret Witmer were always
appreciated."

The Hanover Community Chorus

As part of the celebration activities commemorating the
150th Anniversary of the Incorporation of Hanover, a
community chorus was formed to provide nightly concerts
during the celebration held in mid-September 1915. The
choir was composed of over 130 voices under the direction
of Miss C.M. Cramp. Their sound must have been inspiring
as an out-of-town visitor who sat in on their dress rehearsal
cited in the September 10, 1915 <u>Evening Sun</u> ,

How the little lady who directs this hugh
choir succeeded in training those voices to
blend so beautifully in so short a time will
forever remain a mystery. The work
accomplished is worthy of the most skilled in
the art of all arts- chorus direction. Perhaps
it is the inherent spirit of the occasion which
has lent itself to assisting Miss Cramp in the
particularly pleasing accomplishment.

Whatever the secret, the Community Choir
sings as I would imagine the angels to sing,
with a feeling and vim born of love and
sincerity and a desire to impress the hearts
and minds of those who are to be our guests
Centennial Week. Truly, I thought such
music comes only from souls that feel the

deeper meaning of the words their voices
sing.

The Hanover Choral Club

The Hanover Choral Club was organized in the fall of 1935
by a group of Hanoverians intent on stirring up a greater
interest in vocal music in the community. It was a mixed
voice chorus of about 40 people under the direction of W.
Richard Weagley with Virgil K. Fox as accompanist.

The group gave two concerts annually. Their most notable
concert was their performance of "The Holy Child " by Eric.
Gritten. It was the first rendition of the cantata in the United
States.   On several occasions the Choral Club appeared as
guest artists, performing four or five selections, at the K.of P.
Band's annual spring concert.

The Hanover Elks Chorus

One of Hanover's most notable choruses, one that would
gain national recognition, began as a quartet and then
multiplied into the Hanover Elks Chorus. The original quartet
was composed of Bill Frock, second tenor, Harold Price,
baritone, "Brownie" Nassivera, bass, Paul Worchester, first
tenor and director, and Homer Meredith as accompanist.
According to Paul Worchester, this group gathered whenever
they had the urge and sang together for their own pleasure.
After a few weeks of working together, word got around that
they were very good and they were invited to sing at a
meeting at the Eichelberger High School.

The original quartet members were also all members of the
Hanover Elks Lodge. In the days following their first
performance, other men approached Worchester wanting to
join the group. The Hanover Elks Chorus was formed.

Membership in the Elks Lodge was a pre-requisite . Previous musical training or the ability to read music was optional. A commitment to regular rehearsals and Paul Worchester's directing style was mandatory. Lester Hamme was chosen as the group's accompanist.

While the group bore the Elk's name, they never received any financial support from the Lodge. The original quartet swelled to over forty members. They decided that rehearsals would be held year-round every Monday evening on the third floor of the Baltimore Street Lodge. Since several members were in the retail business, rehearsals could not begin until after 9:00 PM and lasted well past 11:00 PM.

Donations from the chorus members made it possible to buy their first music from Bob Menchey. The group decided to have uniforms. Greenabaums made tuxedos available at a reasonable price and each man paid for his own outfit. Lawrence Sheppard provided the dress shoes at no cost.

Rehearsals continued on a regular basis and soon the group was overwhelmed with invitations to perform. While they never charged for a performance, they did accept donations. Their expenses for music and travel costs were funded in this manner. Their musical repertoire numbered over 40 selections including religious , patriotic, and popular tunes. All music was memorized for performance.

The Grand Elks Lodge had been holding National Lodge Chorus competitions for several years when the Hanover Elks Chorus made its debut in the competition at the National Convention in 1946. The Hanover Elks Chorus won its first National Championship that year with five more Championships to follow. Their National Championship trophies are still on display in the Hanover Elks Lodge showcase today.

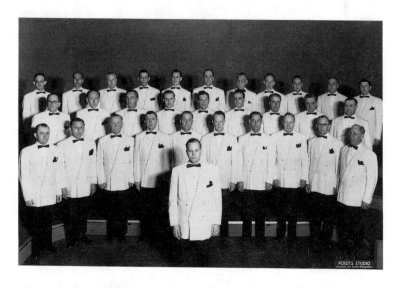

The Hanover Elks Chorus circa 1950. Center, Paul
Worchester, Director. Front Row (l - r): Robert Bunty,
William Frock, Harold Price, Howard Finley, Ralph
Hamme, Robert "Jack" Matthews, Hery Bollinger,
Mac Messinger,_____, Ambrose Klunck. Second
Row (l - r): Alfred Schott, Walter Geilser, Hammon Dell,
Marvin Stine, Fred Weaver, Ed Conrad, Lester Hamme,
accompanist, Homer Meredith, Horace Stine. Third Row (l
- r): Bill Showwalter, Fred MacDonald, _____,
Edgar Orndorff, Tom Smyser, George Swartz, Maurice
"Brownie" Nassivara , Jake Wirt, Mike Hearn,Norman
Becker, William Bowman.

The chorus sang for every kind of group imaginable; civic groups, church groups, state conventions, and veteran's groups, just to name a few. They traveled to New York City where they sang in national competition in the Grand Ballroom of the Waldorff Astoria. Paul Worchester remembers that just before going on for that performance Horace Stein, one of the group's strongest voices, ripped his tuxedo pants from the crotch to the waist band. Worchester darted into an office adjacent to the stage, grabbed a stapler, and stapled Steins pants together just before they walked on stage. The group went on to win another National Championship there.

The group also performed in St. Louis, Chicago, Milwaukee, and Miami. Former chorus member Bill Bowman recalls marching in the Elks Convention Parade in Miami in sweltering heat and humidity in his tuxedo while his feet sizzled in his leather dress shoes on the hot asphalt. Harold Price, one of the original quartet members, suffered a heart attack in the same parade. He recovered and sang in later performances.

By 1952 some of the chorus members wives joined the chorus and a women's group was formed. Several concerts were given featuring men's , women's, and mixed chorus groups selections. Bowman recalls, " The music just gave me such a thrill. Paul got us to work hard and for a group of just 'hometown' guys and girls, we were pretty darn good."

A Community Male Chorus, with former members the Elks Chorus as its nucleus, provided the vocal entertainment at the town's Bicentennial Celebration in 1963. The 60-voice chorus performed songs from the Civil War period and was directed by Paul F. Worchester. Mrs. Leona Klunk played the organ in addition to piano accompaniment by Lester L.

Hamme. Special arrangements of most of the numbers were done by Robert Meredith. While members of the Elks Chorus anchored subsequent community choral groups, the group disbanded in the late 1950's.

The Hanover Standardbred Barbershop Chorus

The Hanover Choral Club was plagued by a shortage of male voices. Almost every rehearsal announcement carried a call for more men to join the club. The Elks Chorus dissolved due to a lack of first tenors. Yet , one of Hanover's oldest vocal groups is the all-male "Hanover Standardbred Barbershop Chorus".

Today's 48-member chorus had its origins in the summer of 1965 when Earl Bittinger, lead; Robert Carthew, tenor; David Landis, baritone; and Gary Forry, bass, formed a quartet and began singing Barbershop-style music in Hanover. Robert Carthew had previous experience with Barbershop choruses and spearheaded the impetus to start a chorus in the area. While the Haover Elks Chorus had chosen to stir clear of Barbershop harmonies, this group embraced them and made them their own.

According to the group's chapter history, Barbershop Harmony is a style of unaccompanied vocal music characterized by consonant four part chords or every melody note. Barbershop music features major and minor chords and barbershop seventh chords(major and Minor sevenths) resolving primarily on the circle of fifths.

About 15 men attended the organizational meeting in 1966 and the following officers were elected; Merle Miller, President; Richard Weaver, Vice-President; David Landis, Secretary; Gerald Orndorff, Treasurer; Norman Blouse,

Business Manager; Ray Huff, Claude Forry, and Earl Bittinger, Board Members; and Robert Carthew as Director.

The chorus was originally chartered as the "Chorus of the Conewago" . But in 1973, the chapter voted to change its name to the "Hanover Standardbred Barbershop Chorus". Since 1968, the chorus has presented its annual concert to the public on the fourth Saturday in September. In addition, the chorus now boasts three registered quartets; the "Penn Villains"; the "Sound Board" ; and the "Appletones".

The Hanover Oratorio Society- Revived

The 1960's also saw the resurrection of the Hanover Oratorio Society. This choral group was dedicated to performing only classic Oratorio works, much as their predecessor had performed fifty years earlier. According to Jesse Betlyon, the new group's first conductor was Esther Becker. Membership in the group ranged from 40 to 75 people with rehearsals and performances rotating among the town's churches. Rehearsals were held every Tuesday or Thursday evening, depending on the host church's choir rehearsal schedule. Betlyon took on the directorship after Becker. The society gave two performances annually until it was disbanded in the mid 1980's.

The chorus seldom varied its fare. Oratorios such as Handel's "Messiah" and Mendelsohn's "Elijah" were community favorites. One exception from their strict oratorio program was their concert for the Bicentennial Wagon Train that encamped at the the Hanover YMCA tract on George Street on its way to Philadelphia to celebrate the nation's 200th birthday.

Jesse Betlyon directed the group of approximately 40 voices with Susan Platt serving as accompanist. The Oratorio

Society serenaded the cross-continental wagoneers with a group of selection entitled "Songs the Washington Knew". This collection was originally compiled to celebrate the 200th Anniversary of George Washington's Birthday. Their finale was Beethoven's " The Heavens are Telling" .

To celebrate the national Bicentennial, the Hanover Area Bicenrennial Committee staged a "Night of Music" at Sheppard and Myers Athletic Field. This effort was spearheaded by Jack Schuler, Paul Worchester, and the area band directors. Approximately 700 area residents participated in the production. A large Honor Band and a 208-voice adult community choir gave a concert saluting the Armed Forces. Members of the Hanover Oratorio Society anchored the chorus. Also on the program was a combined community orchestra, a 200- voice children's' choir, and the popular AARP Kitchen Band, composed of senior citizens from the community.

The Hanover Community Singers

Since its earliest history, Hanover's churches have held combined services to mark special church holidays or community events. In the 1930's the Hanover Ministerial Association held a series of union twilight services in Wirt Park each Sunday evening during July and August. Music was an integral part of those services. The announcement printed in the Evening Sun for the August 25th, 1934 service noted that several choral selections would be offered by the St. Matthew Lutheran Church Choir under the direction of J. Herbert Springer, the prelude would be offered by the orchestra of the Intermediate Department of St. Matthew's Sunday School under the direction of Paul A. Horner, and a concert by the Lyric Band of Hanover under the direction of H. W. Swartzbaugh would immediately follow the service.

It was after working together in an Ecumenical Service at Lohr's United Methodist Church in January 1987 that Scott G. Fredericks and Karen L. Buckwalter conceived the idea of forming a mixed-voice community chorus- The Hanover Community Singers.

As it happened, Buckwalter was to play the organ for the Ecumenical service as well as direct the choir, which was composed of choir members from the area churches. Because of the location of the organ console, she could not see to direct the large choir. She asked Scott Fredericks to direct the choir while she accompanied. Singers, director, and accompanist meshed so well that the now 180-voice chorus is still performing to standing-room only audiences a decade later.

In addition to Fredericks as President and Buckwalter as Secretary, the Singers first Executive Committee included: Donald Lawrence, Board Member; Beverly Stevens, Librarian; Lisa Smith, Program Assistant; Margie Noel, Treasurer; and Linda Cole, Financial Assistant.

The Hanover Community Singers hold two concerts annually at St. Matthew Lutheran Church- one at Christmas and one in the spring. Three performances of each concert are given. The chorus has also performed Pops Concert at the Hanover High School, performed at the National Pageant for Peace in Washington, DC , sang at the town's July 4th Celebration at Moul Field with the Lyric Band, and had their Christmas concerts broadcast on Hanover Cable television.

Director Scott G. Fredericks says of the group,

We, the members of the Hanover
Community Singers, come from all walks of
life, all musical abilities, and all ages. We

represent this community, not just the trained musical community.

We began as Christians united in song to our Lord and this spirit has brought us through ten years of offering our gift of song to the community.

Our audiences participate with the singers. We hope our concerts are not just for the audience, but we include them in our excitement, sorrow, prayer, laughter, joy and tears.

Our music is an extension of who we are as humans, who we are as Christians, and who we are as members of this community.

The bell choir at Trinity United Church of Christ, known as The Trinity Ringers, has performed in three of the Hanover Community Singers' concerts. Like their counterparts in other churches, they ring their handbells mostly for worship services. However, members have also attended handbell conferences and this choir hosted a bell choir festival in Trinity's Fellowship Hall.

Director of The Trinity Ringers and the Minister of Music at Trinity United Church of Christ is Karen L. Buckwalter. Mrs. Buckwalter is a graduate of the Westminster Choir College and holds an artist's diploma in organ from the Curtiss Institute in Philadelphia. She is nationally known as a composer of handbell and choral music. Her handbell music has been recorded in both the United States and Japan.

Special Concerts and Players

Hanover is indeed a musical center.
Besides our own musical organizations, we
have been honored with a visit from ten
organ men this season.

Hanover Spectator
June 9, 1880

The Telephone Concerts

Hanoverians have always gone to great lengths for their
musical entertainment. They even extended the original
meaning of "party-line" when telephone service was first
introduced to the area by the Hanover Telephone Company
in 1894.

In an article in the September 7, 1934, Evening Sun, Mr.
T. J. O'Neill, who was closely associated with the Hanover
telephone system, recalled that early in 1893 Hanover had
only one phone. The private line operated in the home of Dr.
R. N. Meisenhelder with one Hanover phone in Abbottsbown
and one in East Berlin.

Realizing the value of a telephone system in Hanover, Mr.
O'Neill contacted Mart Beuhler, manager of the
Pennsylvania Bell Telephone Company in Harrisburg,
concerning having the company place an exchange in
Hanover. Beuhler replied that the town was too small to
support an exchange. He suggested that the people of
Hanover operate their own system.

Determined to have telephone service in Hanover, O'Neill spearheaded the formation of the Hanover Telephone Company. The company erected the poles, strung the wires, and purchased the phones that were to be rented or sold to subscribers. The company purchased the latest battery operated phones on the market from the Western Electric Construction Company of Chicago.

As an inducement to prospective subscribers of the telephone service, musical concerts were given over the telephone each weekday evening at 9 o'clock and sacred concerts were presented on Sundays. Local papers reported that Hanoverians enjoyed using their telephones to listen to these varied musical presentations. The following are excerpts from the Evening Herald:

December 8, 1894

About fifty of the telephone subscribers were entertained last night by some very fine vocal and instrumental music sent over the wires. Soprano and bass solos, a banjo, a music box, and a gramophone furnished entertainment from about 10 o'clock until almost midnight. A large number of the lines were connected with the exchange and the sounds were heard with great distinction.

December 10, 1894

Another concert was given over the telephone on Saturday night. There were several solos by well known soprano and bass singers, and also cornet solos by Irvin Naill.

There was also a concert given last night.
Among a number of good selections sung
was a trio by Harry Stauffer, Michael Hoke,
and Mrs. Harry Smith. There was also some
excellent whistling by a young lady of Middle
Street. These concerts have become quite
popular.

While the entertainment served its purpose of obtaining
new subscribers, it proved costly from a battery standpoint.
While listeners-in all over the system, which also included
New Oxford, Menges Mills, and Spring Grove, enjoyed the
music, the battery operated phones were drained of power.

Sousa Comes to Hanover

Hanoverians love a good band concert. Whether by their
own musicians or by a touring band, a capacity crowd can
be expected if the concert program sounds promising.
While countless bands have played in the Old Concert Hall,
the Hanover Opera House, the Park Theater, and in the high
school and churches, at least one of Hanover's most popular
band presentations warrents highlighting.

On April 13 , 1915, the "March King" John Philip Sousa,
his band, and special soloists appeared at the Hanover Opera
House for an afternoon concert. Promotional articles
appeared on the front page of the Hanover Independent daily
for a week prior to the performance. An earlier reference was
made to Sousa having traveled through Hanover on his way
to give a concert in Baltimore in the late 1890's, but no
mention is made of his having given a concert in Hanover at
that time.

Details of the 1915 concert are profuse. In addition to the
concert band, Virginia Post, soprano, Margel Gluck,

violinist, and Herbert L. Clark, cornetist appeared as soloists. The program included Sousa standards such as "El Capitan", "King Cotton", and the "Stars and Stripes Forever". The band also performed excerpts from Wagner's opera "Tristan and Isola". The community seemed to be as captivated by the man as they were by his music. An excerpt from the April 6, 1915 issue of the Hanover Independent reads, "Sousa is not an experiment. He is like Mark Twain in the library or Edison with the telephone and phonograph. He is the one and only of his kind."

Opera Stars

In the 1920's and 30's, Hanover annually celebrated "Music Week". Photos and feature articles about musical organizations of the past were published in the papers and free concerts by the town's bands and other musical groups filled a week-long schedule.

During "Music Week" in May 1935, Miss Suzanne Keener performed in concert at the Opera House. Miss Keener was a coloratura soprano with the Metropolitan Opera Company. The May 8th issue of the Record Herald noted, " Her voice is of a superb timbre absolutely perfect in intonation and under magnificent control. Her pianissimo in the highest register is a thing of rare musical beauty and she sings without effort and with clear enunciation."

Today, Hanover can proudly lay claim to a homegrown opera star of world-wide acclaim. Karen Bureau is a renowned dramatic soprano who has sung on stages from Germany to Hong Kong and from the New York City Metropolitan Opera to the Victoria State Opera in Sidney, Australia.

Bureau's voice, which has both a high range and a heavy quality, is a voice perfectly suited for Wagnerian opera. According to a quote that Bureau made to the Evening Sun in December 1997, there are perhaps only eight women in the world capable of singing the role of Brunnhilde in Wagner's epic opera, "De Ring des Nibelungen", better known as "The Ring Cycle". She is one of them. Bureau returned to her hometown in late 1997 after completing a seven year contract with Staatstheater Hanover , an opera house in Germany in 1993.

The Little German Band

Organized in the 1920's, Gobrecht's Little German Band was in considerable demand for many years, appearing at county fairs, reunions, banquets and flea markets throughout the southeastern part of Pennsylvania and Maryland. The initial band included William, Edward J., and Joseph Gobrecht along with Paul Stauffer, Edward Warner, and Ralph Myers.

By 1952 the group was composed of Edward J., Emory, and William Gobrecht, Paul Stauffer, and Franklin Leinhart-trumpet, trombone, tuba, and two clarinets. The group played march music, polkas, and traditional German tunes. It was their German repertoire that landed them a spot on the "Der Alt Dulmaisher" show early in the history of radio station WHVR.

Advertising salesman at the station, Vernon Ferster, made a pitch to Leinhart Brothers Furniture to become one of the first sponsors for the new station. In the course of his conversation with Mr. Leinhart, a Pennsylvania Dutch program was mentioned. Mr. Leinhart like the idea and enthusiastically agreed to sponsor a fifteen minute program. The program was to include news and special items of interest spoken in Pennsylvania Dutch with two commercial spots for Leinhart Brothers Furniture.

Since Ferster was the only member of the radio staff who spoke Pennsylvania Dutch, the program fell on his shoulders. He latched upon the formula of first giving a synopsis of the program in English, and then delivering the Pennsylvania Dutch version. Because of their repertoire of German tunes, Fester had the Little German Band record their most popular melodies. These songs were a big hit with the listening audience. Ferster used one of their numbers midway through almost every program. This broke the program into two parts and to gave "Der Alt Dulmaishder" an opportunity to catch his breath.

The Hanover String Quartet

In 1976, Charmine Noel, Eunice Heistand, Clyde Mummert, and Martha Lippy formed a string quartet to play chamber music for their own pleasure. But its hard to keep a good thing a secret in Hanover, and soon the group was sought-after to play at small, intimate gatherings. This group still plays beautiful chamber music and is in great demand today. They are the Hanover String Quartet.

Eunice Heistand no longer plays with them. Clyde Mummert passed away in October 1997. In addition to his early guidance in forming the group, Mummert was also the teacher for two of the group's present members. Currently the quartet is composed of Charmine Noel, Debra Zumbrum, Diane Hoffman , and Martha Lippy.

The quartet was an ideal candidate to perform in the first music series sponsored by the Hanover Public Library. The concert, held in the library's Pennsylvania Room, provided the perfect environment for a small group, playing quality

classical music. The group and the setting were such a
perfect match, that the group has performed in this series on
an annual basis.

Since the group is small and very mobile, they have
performed in a variety of locations and settings ranging from
outdoor weddings in woodlands and meadows, to the
Pennsylvania State Capital Rotunda, where they played for
Governor Robert Casey. One of their most challenging
performances was given from a loft in a horse barn where
they sat perched about twenty feet above the audience.

Duo Times Two

Hanover has had a myriad of small vocal groups, dance
bands, and ensembles over the years. Time restraints limit
seeking out every one, but a few can be named to show the
variety and depth of talent of many of these local groups.

In 1930, the Tin Can Quartet, composed of Francis
Conrad, Jamie Conrad, Jim Roth, and Jake Wierman, sang
locally and performed the "National Bo" commercial on
Baltimore radio. Jim Roth taught his daughters to sing
harmony and "The Roth Sisters" sang on WHVR every
Saturday morning. The York Street Garage was their
sponsor. There was also the Hanover Oahu Guitar Band, the
Boys Club Serenaders, the Range Riders, the Hawaiian
Sharps, the Melo-Tones, the Zinn Weeks Band, banjo duo
Hank Larkin and Dwight Alcott, and the Katzen Jammers,
just to name a few.

Popular concerts of a more recent genre in Hanover have
been those performed by four women who combined their
piano playing virtuosity to form a two-piano/ eight-hand
group known as Duo Times Two. There are probably fewer

than a dozen eight-hand piano performing groups in the world; fewer still made up entirely of women.

The members of Duo Times Two are Mary Ann Fiery, Joan Bowman, Joyce Elsner, and Nancy Leister. Prior to their collaboration in 1992, they had given concerts as separate duos, Fiery and Bowman having performed together since 1972 and Elsner and Leister since 1988.

Like so many others in Hanover's past, this group was motivated to use their talents to benefit their community. Duo Times Two played its official debut concert as a fund-raiser to benefit the Adams-Hanover Counseling Services. This was followed by many subsequent concerts given in New York, North Carolina, Pennsylvania, Alabama, and an additional benefit concert for the Counseling Services.

During the summer of 1997, the members of Duo Times Two and the musicians and directors of seven other local groups combined their talents in the inaugural recording of the series, "Christmas in Hanover". The ten selection compact disk or tape featured special holiday music from each group. Proceeds from the sale of "Christmas in Hanover" were donated to the Hanover Area Council of Churches. A full listing of the recording participants , producer, and engineer can be found in Appendix IV.

The Austin Organ

This instrument was built and dedicated
that its music might resound to the Glory of
God and to the uplifting of God's people in
worship. It was also the desire of the donor
and the earnest hope of the designer-organist
that its beautiful and glorious tone might
give inspiration and pleasure to many beyond
the membership of the St. Matthew
congregation.

> Pamphlet St. Matthew
> Lutheran Church concerning
> their Austin Organ

A gem in the crown of Hanover's musical community is
the Austin pipe organ at St. Matthew Lutheran Church on
Chestnut St. In 1931, with its 12,729 pipes, Hanover could
boast of having the largest mono-console controlled church
organ in the world. Today, although out-ranked in size
worldwide by a handful of organs , this organ is still
distinguished by its exceptionally exquisite tonal qualities.

No records exist as to exactly when pipe organs came to
Hanover. Records in Philadelphia do verify that the first pipe
organs in America were made by Pennsylvania Germans as
early as 1704.   There is also evidence to suggest that small
Tanneberg organs, made in Lititz at the David Tanneberg
Organ Works, were purchased for St. Matthew Lutheran
Church and Emmanuel Reformed Church of Hanover in the
1790's.

The purchase price for such an instrument at that time was three hundred pounds currency, or about fifteen hundred dollars.

Records do confirm a pipe organ at St. Matthew when the congregation built its church on Chestnut St. in 1807. Some of the literature suggests that during that same year, a new organ built by local organ-builder Adam Ault was installed in the Emmanuel Reform Church. Since the organ bore the name "Bachman", an organ builder who was Tanneberger's successor, these references must be considered dubious. St. Matthew Lutheran Church replaced their organ again in 1879.

The committee who purchased this new organ included the Rev. J.C. Koller, pastor, William Kump, George Kleinfelter, Sr., H. W. Heilecker, and J. P. Schultz. This organ served the congregation through a dozen organists and eight different choir directors. This organ was replaced by a more modern Moller organ around 1916.

In 1924 St. Matthew Lutheran Church completed their fifth church edifice in their long, continuous history. Organized in April 1743, it is the oldest Lutheran congregation west of the Susquehanna River. Befitting the majestic gray stone Gothic designed church, a new organ was conceived by church organist J. Herbert Springer and brought to life by the benevolence of Mrs. Clara Glatfelter Moul.

Springer was an avid reader and researcher by nature. It was through much of his own study of registration that the concept for the great organ developed in his mind. He alone determined that the organ must be built by the Austin Organ Company. The Austin Organ Company was noted for building the outer case of its organs of wood, while using metal, wherever feasible, for the movable parts; wood being much more susceptible to the stresses caused by changes in ambient temperature and humidity. He also insisted that they build a four-manual console instead of five, as was the tradition at the time. He felt that a five-console organ was excellent as a show-piece for theaters, but it was an abomination to an organist. The extra console just got in his way.

The new organ was under construction for several months in the factory of the Austin Organ Company, Hartford, Conn., before being loaded on three railroad cars and transported to Hanover. According to the Record Herald, June 6, 1924,

> Two carloads of material, each weighing 27,000 pounds, have already arrived and the final carload will be shipped this month. This material includes more than 4500 wood and metal pipes, the smallest half an inch long and the largest 32 feet long; bellows, air boxes, chests, cables, expression control shutters and blowers. One immense blower, ran by a 15 horse-power motor, will supply air at various pressures for the major part of the organ, and a smaller blower will serve the big Tuba.

The original instrument had a scope of 87 speaking stops. Some of the largest pipes weighed over 400 pounds each. Fred Rassman of the Austin Organ Company supervised the entire installation and tuning of the organ.

Originally dedicated in 1925, the organ was expanded by 2800 pipes in 1929 and again in 1931 with almost 5000 more additional pipes. This brought the total number of pipes to 12,729. Mrs. Moul enthusiastically supported these enlargements which also required building a grill ceiling over the chancel to house the Solo Chamber.

Following the dedicatory program for the newly expanded organ in 1931, Springer wrote to the Austin Organ Company to congratulate them on their fine workmanship. The company published his letter along with his picture in their company ad in the January 1, 1932 issue of <u>The Diapason</u> . A portion of his letter reads:

> It gives me great pleasure to congratulate you on your overwhelming success with the St. Matthew's organ. I am quite of the opinion that it is not only one of the largest organs ever built, but just as surely one of the very finest. Hundreds of organists who attended my dedicatory recital on December 1st and many from far and near who have played the organ have praised it with the greatest enthusiasm...

> If the mechanism of this great organ were not so simple it would be uncanny. Visiting organists have expressed amazement that any console containing 237 stops, many couplers and other controls, 90 adjustable pistons (52 of which have second touch), and the entire piston action can be so small. My only comment can be that I believe no other organ builder in the world could have done it.

J. Herbert Springer served as organist and choirmaster for 52 years at St. Matthew Lutheran Church and continued to make additions and changes to the organ's original design during most of his tenure. More additions and changes have been made over the years to the organ with the console being rebuilt again in 1964. Today the organ has a total of 14,341 pipes. It contains 231 ranks, 239 speaking stops, 48 couplers, 90 adjustable pistons and a manual disposition of : I Choir, II Great, Great Echo, III Swell, IV Solo, and Solo Echo. Wind is supplied by four blowers with a combined output of 37 horsepower that supply pressures varying from 7" to 20".

Early in 1971, a Schulmerich 25 Flemish Bell "Arlington" Carillon was installed in the church and connected to the organ console. This provided for manual playing of the bells. They could be sounded both inside and outside of the church. The bronze Flemish bells which constituted the heart of this instrument evolved for cast bells, in that each Flemish bell noted consisted of two bells. The "A" bell provided the minor partial structure while the "B" bell provided the major partial. Blended, they formed the complete partial (overtone) structure found in large, tuned cast bells. This carillon was given to the church as a memorial to Leonelle Schue Worchester by the Paul Worchester Family.

By 1988 the Schulmerich Carillon had become increasingly difficult to maintain and repair. It was replaced with a digital Chronobell Maas-Rowe Carillon and a 198 Grand Symphony Carillon. St. Matthew Church's Minister of Music, Scott G. Fredericks, collaborated with the company's design specialists to configure this unique instrument.

The Maas-Rowe Carillon is composed of individually tuned metal rods, similar to the rods in a grandfather clock. A computer device transfers the music on the organ to the rods which are housed in cabinets in the church's basement. A transducer detects the vibrations of each bell and then supplies the appropriate electrical signal to powerful amplifiers. Speakers in the church tower sends the music out and across Hanover.

The basic Maas-Rowe unit is a 74-bell Symphonic Carillon consisting of 37 minor English Bells and 37 major English Bells. In addition, the Carillon at St. Matthew Lutheran Church has 26 Bourden Bells, 37 Flemish Bells, 12 Upper Minor Bells, and 49 Harp-Celeste Bells. It is one of the largest Carillon ever designed and installed by the Maas-Rowe Company.

The basic Maas-Rowe Carillon unit was given to the church as a memorial to the family of Mr. and Mrs. George F. Rohrbaugh by Frysinger Brown Rohrbaugh. All additional bells were memorialized by members and friends of the congregation. The new Maas-Rowe Carillon was dedicated on Sunday, September 25, 1988 at a special concert given by renowned organist James A. Dale.

Since Mr. Springer's tenure, the great Austin organ has been under the care of three other talented organists serving the St. Matthew congregation. James E. Derr served as organist from 1968 until 1974. Thomas W. D. Guthrie was organist for the next six years. Since 1980, Scott G. Fredericks has served in the capacity of Minister of Music. Margie R. Lee was hired in March 1996 as the church's Associate Minister of Music to assist with its expanded music ministry .

In 1982 the church council declared the organ to be complete. At that time the organ was valued at 1.5 million dollars.

The Austin Organ at St. Matthew Lutheran Church, 30
West Chestnut Street, Hanover , PA.

Menchey Means Music

The philosophy of Menchey Music Service
is to provide a full service music outlet to
musical customer of all ages, talents, and
musical tastes...

Our policy is to provide honest advise and
top-qualiaty products and service to our
customers. We sell stuff, buy stuff, rent
stuff, and fix stuff. Whether you are a
beginner, a professional musician, a baby-
boomer wanna-get-back-into-it, a school
music director, a choral director, a member
of a traveling band, a retired former musician
or whatever, Menchey Music Service can
service your musical needs.

Statement of Company
Philosophy, Menchey Music Service
http://www.menchey.com/philos.html

While several music dealers in Hanover, Westminster,
York and Harrisburg have sold instruments and printed
music to Hanover's varied musical groups, none have
serviced the local musical community more completely for
the past sixty years than Menchey Music Service. Founded
in 1936 by Robert Menchey, the company has grown to
become Central Pennsylvania's dominant full service music
dealer. The company also has one of the most extensive
printed music libraries in the country. Today, via the internet
and through professional references, Menchey Music Service
supplies musical services to the entire mid-Atlantc region and
beyond.

As a young man, Bob Menchey was an excellent trombonist who played in the York Symphony and directed the Sunday School Church Orchestra at St. Matthew Lutheran Church. He made his living teaching instrumental music lessons, charging fifty cents for a half-hour lesson. He also collected $5 for each band rehearsal he directed in the area.

Bob was quick to recognize the need for a local business that could supply instrunments, perform repairs , and procure printed music for the numerous community bands, orchestras, and vocal groups in the York and Adams County areas and neighboring Carroll County. He started his venture in 1936 when he sold a saxophone for a $10 profit, which he re-invested into inventory to launch Menchey Music Service. His first "store" was located at 312, Second Avenue, Hanover, in what had previously been his mother's sewing room.

Driven by perseverance and aided by his charasmatic personality, Menchey gained a reputation as a reliable supplier of good quality instruments, accessories, and printed music. He was one of only a handfull of music suppliers who could get printed music in the early 40's. Bob recalls, "During the war years there was a shortage of paper. I was able to get copies of the Schaum Piano Methods series, even though they were printed on newsprint paper. No one could get any copies of the Thompson Methods."

Stocking both a variety of musical instruments, their accessories, and printed music, dictated a need for more room and Menchey Music Service re-located to 513 Baltimore Street in 1941. The new location had twice the floor space of the previous "sewing room" store.

Ray Hamm came to work for Bob Menchey in 1948. Hamm worked as a route salesman visiting schools and band directors on a weekly basis. Hamm and Menchey Music formed a working relationship that would last for years and set one of the cornerstones of the Menchey Music Service business- the school music program.

Acting as a liason between the store and the band directors, Hamm offered beginning band and orchestra students Menchey instruments on a rental plan, as well as sheet music, accessories, and minor repairs. He helped establish Menchey Music Services' reputation for reliablity and service. Today, thirty percent of their business is derived from their band rental program. The company employs four road representatives to regularly service schools in Pennsylvania, Maryland , and parts of West Virginia.

By 1950 the store was expanded again with a move to 18 York Street. It was around this time that the block and circle logo with the slogan "Menchey Means Music" that has become synonymous with the store was adopted. Wanting a complete music store, Bob added pianos to his inventory. Rather, it was a piano, since the supplier would only let him have one instrument for display. Once it was sold, another would be shipped. He sold his first console piano to a lady in Gettysburg and his first baby-grand piano to Trinity United Church of Christ in Hanover. The baby-grand is still in service today.

Piano sales are cyclical. Yet, Hanoverians have always privately owned a disportionately high number of pianos and organs. In the boon years of piano sales, Menchey's piano supplier estimated that based on the demographics of the community, the store could expect to sell 13 pianos that year- Menchey sold 123. Today, acoustical pianos and organs share floor space with digital keyboards and the latest in supplies for keyboard labs in the schools

About this same time the Menchey Music Workshops were launched. The son of piano methods guru John Thompson was the director for the first workshop held in a hotel across from the Baltimore Street store. It was held in January 1948 and a treacherous ice storm had glazed over the roads the previous night. Yet, a dozen piano teachers managed to attend. As the store's sales of printed music mushroomed, more publishers saw Menchey's Music Workshops as a prime sales tool. Many of the early workshops were targeted towards band directors.

For the past twenty years Menchey Music Service has hosted a church music workshop at St. Matthew Lutheran Church. Upwards to 750 church musicians from the tri-state area attend this annual event to preview and sing the latest church anthem music and meet with church music composers, arrangers, and publishing representatives. Church music directors can order the music directly from the publishers that day at a considerable discount.

Sales of printed music now make up more than thirty percent of Menchey's sales volume. Fifty percent of those sales are in choral music. The store takes pride in having one of the most complete sheet music libraries in the country. Menchey employs specialists in each specific area of their sheet music sales- choral, instrumental, and popular/piano.

Bursting at the seams with inventory, the store was moved again to a mansion-style home at 430 Carlisle Street. The bedrooms were converted to studios and the wrap-around porch was glassed in to serve as a piano showroom. By now the Korean Conflict was in full- swing and while pianos were

still selling well , federally mandated price controls held
down profits .

The public's musical taste cranked up a beat and the store
acquired home and church organs along with guitars to
service the trend . While Bob's musical passions leaned
towards the sales of band instruments and fine keyboards, he
approached the guitar business with the same dedication and
service he afforded his favorites. Menchey Music Service
was the second Gibson guitar dealer in York County and one
of the earliest Fender dealers in the country. Today the store
stocks electric and acoustic six and twelve string guitars,
bass guitars, banjos. Mandolins, and ukuleles.

Menchey Music Service moved to its present location at 80
Wetzel Drive in Hanover on August 15, 1988. The Carlisle
Street facility now serves as a warehouse. Since 1995, the
company has also opened stores in York and Lancaster.

In 1995, Bob's grandson, Joel R. Menchey, took over as
President and CEO of Menchey Music Service. Joel is a
hybrid of musician and businessman. Although musical
instruments have become more customized, digitalized, and
computerized and the virtual store on the internet has
weighed in as a viable shopping alternative, Joel Menchey
plans to follow his grandfather's formula for success in the
music business. Always give the customer full service and
change with the times.

Halls, Houses and Theaters

Every community can be judged by its
houses of entertainment. It has been said
that the worth of a man is to be judged by
the manner in which he spends his idle hours.
The man who finds time during the hours
when he is not working, for the better things
of life and time to improve his mind, is the
man who becomes a blessing to the
community in which he lives...

The Record Herald
September 22, 1928

Hanover's houses of entertainment, by themselves, never
contributed a solitary note to any musical production. But,
the location, style, and character of each of these edifaces
colored the musical memories of the audiences who attended
performances there. While the town's earliest performances
and concerts were held in either churches or private homes,
the public's appetite for the performing arts soon required a
facility capable of seating not just one hundred people, but
several hundred persons.

The Old Concert Hall

The Old Concert Hall, located on the southwest angle of
Center Square, was Hanover's sole amusement hall for
several decades. The Hall was originally a school building
that had been owned by Prof. William Tell Barnitz. The
building was purchased in 1859 by Dr. Vincent E. S. Eckert
who renovated it to accommodate an audience of six

hundred people. The Hall was used as an Armory for the Hanover Infantry and the Marion Riflemen.

The front of the hall was two stories. The frontage onto the square was only about twelve feet, but off the square, it widened to 30 feet. The hall extended 125 feet in length, running south, with a stage at the south end and dressing rooms under the stage.

There were two doors in the front, the first opening to the stairway to the second floor, and the other entering into the lobby. The lobby was 10 feet by 15 feet in dimensions with a ticket office in the left-hand corner and the door to the auditorium to the right. The ticket seller could sell a ticket, step around the corner to receive the ticket from the patron as he entered the auditorium, and then return to the ticket box and dispose of the same ticket again.

The Hall served as the concert hall for the Citizens Band. The Band practiced twice a week, on Tuesday and Thursday evenings and always drew a large audience. The Hall was located next to Jesse Gitt's stable which exuded a peculiar accompanying aroma on warm summer nights. Since most of the townsfolk kept some type of livestock at their own homes, this feature passed virtually unnoticed.

After Dr. Eckert's death, the second story room of the Hall was occupied by M.O. Smith and Harry Bittinger, publishers of the Hanover Weekly Herald and then by Hanover Advance Printing Company. Later the frame structure was considered a fire trap and was removed for the enlargement of the J. W. Gitt Building.

The Opera House

In 1886 the Hanover Market and Town Hall Company purchased property from R. M. Wirt on West Chestnut Street for the purpose of constructing a building that would house a market on the ground floor and an auditorium on the upper floor; or as it was called in those days, a Town Hall.

The large, single-room ground floor was paved and furnished with tables, butcher blocks, and meat racks. While the second floor, with its dual stairway access and domed ceiling, had been lavishly decorated by the eminent Philadelphia artistic designer, W.F. Wise.

The September 7, 1887 of the <u>Hanover Herald</u> devoted an entire front-page column to describing the second floor audience chamber . This description of the dome ceiling alone hints at the elaborate decor gracing the hall over the heads for the butchers, bakers, and candlestick makers on market days.

> The dome is the center of the ceiling design, which is appropriate and most beautiful, comprising a large center panel, surrounded by three oblong panels. Each of these panels has a medallion center, the side ones having music and the front one having dramatic trophies. There is also a medallion with music trophies at each end of the front panel. To the rear of the hall, over the gallery, is a panel more plainly fashioned. All the panels are light pink terra cotta shade, with light buff borders and blue ornaments. The stiles are in cool gray. The dome is a light olive, ornamented with old gold sheets. Its curved sickles of light yellow are also embellished with green palms. About it swings a circular panel of

The Hanover Opera House on West Chestnut Street.

buff, with an illuminated scroll of arabesque
non-descripts. This panel is broken by four
medallions containing portraits of
Shakespere, Schiller, Mozart and Beethoven.
Effective canopy corners in light cream buff,
add to the beauty of the center panel.

With such artistic grandeur, the hall quickly became known
as the Opera House; not the Town Hall.

The Opera House opened on Monday night, September 12,
1887, with the play "Caprice". The lead was played by Miss
Minnie Madden, a distinguished actress from the Lyceum
Theater in New York City. This play had run for 57
consecutive nights at the Lyceum the previous season. While
the Hanover Herald's opening night preview is full of laurels
for the production and the newly constructed hall, it ends with
this premonition: " The success of Hanover's fine Opera
House, of which all should be justly proud, depends on
whether our people have local pride enough to support it."

The Hanover Market and Town Hall Company's business
acumen ran a rather convoluted course which turned out to be
neither very serviceable to the community nor profitable for
the company. In 1912, the company's property was acquired
by D. M. Frey, who conveyed it to the Hanover Opera House
Company, a corporation which had been formed for the
purpose of establishing, maintaining, and opening a theater.
This company eliminated the market from the lower level and
adapted the entire building for production purposes, including
erecting a larger stage.

The Park Theater

Still operating at a loss, in 1919 the theater was sold to the
Hanover Improvement Company. Attorney C. J. Delone

acquired the property and entirely remodel the building in 1931. The old gallery was removed, the lobby enlarged, new restrooms were installed, seating was enlarged to 1000 seats, and a marquee which extended fourteen feet out over the sidewalk was added to the front entrance. These improvements were made to facilitate the installation of modern sound motion picture equipment. The building was re-named the Park Theater.

The new Park Theater showed feature films from Paramount, Metro-Goldwyn-Mayer, and United Artists. It earned its bread and butter by showing three different shows per week with each attraction running for two days. The matinee prices were 10 cents for children and 25 cents for adults. The admission for the evening shows was 15 cents for children and 30 cents for adults.

While the Park Theater became one of Hanover's first moviehouses, the first movie shown in Hanover had been shown almost 25 years earlier in the Opera House on January 18, 1897. The film was shown on an Edison Projectoscope brought in from Chambersburg. A private exhibition was given before the ministers and school teachers of the town, prior to the opening to the public.

The following account of the exhibition appeared in the local paper. While the film did not have a musical theme, the advent of an alternative form of entertainment to the live drama or musical concert would have a permanent impact on the frequency and form of Hanover's musical productions.

> There was a large audience to witness its
> developments and the applause was
> expressive of enthusiasm. The pictures
> shown were true to life in scene and action...
> The excitement of the New York firemen

A wrecking ball of the L & W Demolition Co., Harrisburg, pounds into the walls of the former Park Theater Building at West Chestnut and North Franklin Streets. This building first served as a market house, then as the Hanover Opera House and subsequently as the Park Theater motion picture establishment. The property was acquired by St. Matthew Lutheran Church and the building was razed to make room for the church's Christian Education Building. Photo courtesy of the St. Matthew Lutheran Church Archives.

dashing to a fire and rescuing children from a dwelling... A bath scene at Rockway Beach was marvelously life-like, and one of the most ludicrous pictures was that of a kissing scene in one of the New York theaters between May Irwin and Frank Rice. Every movement of the lips, twitch of the face and sparkle of the eyes could be seen as clearly as though the onlooker stood beside those who were indulging in the osculatory exercises.

The audience who witness the working of this marvelous machine were at first astounded; lost in wonder, then admiration...

The Strand and State Theaters

The arrival of the motion-picture show in almost every sizable town by the late 1920's dictated that entertainment halls now serve the dual purpose of both movie theater and dramatic stage. To those ends the Strand Theater opened in 1927 and the State Theater was opened in 1928. Both of these theaters also contained large organs which were played for special programs, at the start of the film, and sometimes even during the movie. The Strand Theater installed a Page organ which was billed as enabling the organist to play along with any kind of picture from a comedy to the most dramatic; giving each an accurate musical accompaniment to the action as it transpired on the screen.

The Park Theater property on the corner of Franklin and Chestnut Streets was aquired by the congregation of St. Matthew Lutheran Church in 1967. The old theater was demolished to make way for the church's new Christian Education and Administration building in 1968.

With an increased emphasis on secondary school education in the 1930's, many public schools built stages or auditoriums to service student productions. These school stages and once again the local churches, served as hubs for the performing arts for many of the dramatic and musical productions in Hanover for the next sixty years.

Forest Park

While not a concert hall or theater per se, it would be a a a glaring ommission not to include Forest Park in this section. While known to many only as an amusement park, for others, it was the music, the theatrical productions, and the dancing performed there, that made the park swing.

Forest Park was originally called Eichelburger Park which opened to the public in June of 1904. The park was the brain-child of the Board of Directors of the York Street Railroad Company. The Company extended its line by half-a-mile from York Street to a point in Penn Township near the old Toll Gate. The park was to help promote the railroad's business interest by providing a gathering place for social activities. It was assumed that people would need to ride the train to get there. To that end , the Railroad Company transformed a few acres and a clump of trees into a scenic park with flower beds, picnic tables, steel swings with double seats, a croquet ground, horseshoe pits, and a petting zoo.

Well received by the townsfolk , the park flourished . Pre-opening publicity for the 1909 summer season included this excerpt from the May 15th <u>Record Herald</u> , " The skating rink has at great expense been converted into an attractive theatre, fitted up with all the modern requirements...The paraquet, the seating capacity of which is 440, is fitted with the latest style theater chairs. The gallery which is equipped with folding chairs, has a capacity of 200, which with the bleachers will make a capacity of 1000." The theater was opened that season under the direction of the Chauncy Kieffer Stock Company with featured Miss Grace Kieffer as its star performer. Local papers reported that Miss Kieffers gowns were the finest and most costly ever worn by any actress with a traveling stock company.

In 1925 the park was leased by the Railroad Company to Eustace G. Via, Huntingdon, West Virginia who operated the amusement for just one season. Via's permanent mark was the renaming of the park to Forest Grove Park. It quickly became known simply as, Forest Park.

A year later, August G. Karst and Sons, Philadelphia, took over the management of Forest Park. The park would be operated by the Karst family for the next forty years.

August G. Karst celebrated his fifty- first anniversay in the amusement business in 1940. The same year an article about Forest Park appeared in a supplement to the April 29, 1940 Evening Sun in recognition of the 125th anniversary of the incorporation of the Borough of Hanover. This article leaves no doubt as to the quality and quanity of music performed at Forest Park.

> Receiving patronage for the entire county and from Adams and Carroll counties the park offers among many other features: free band concerts, vaudeville acts, and radio entertainment from time to time; mass band concerts every year with 500 men musicians playing.. and dancing Wednesday and Saturday nights in the ballroom to popular orchestras...

Vaudevillian acts were quite the rage on the theater at
Forest Park. Professional players chorus line shown seated
here were all local Hanover girls. Seated fifth from the right
is Catherine Rebecca Wildasin. This photo courtesy of
Nancy Leister whose mother was the chorus line girl seated
fifth from the right.

August G. Garst died in August 1948 and was buried at the Mt. Olivet Cemetry, just a short stroll from his beloved Forest Park. August F. Karst continued operating the park until 1967, but without the senior Garst, the park never seemed to regain the sparkle and vitality of an earlier era.

Morton E. Kalus purchased the park property in 1967. The South Hanover Shopping Center stands there today. Forest Park Hanover, Penna. by Mary Kelly Mills and Harold E. Colestock, is an excellent compilation of the complete history of Forest Park based on local newsprint articles. Copies can be purchased at the Hanover Public Library.

The Eichelberger Performing Arts Center

The Eichelberger Performing Arts Center has undergone several metamorphises. The center section was built in 1896 and the auditorium and gymnasium wings were added in 1933. The facility began as the Eichelberger Academy, then served as the Eichelberger High School and later as the Hanover High and Hanover Middle School. The Hanover School District stopped using the building for educational purposes in 1991. All told, the school's auditorium has been used by Hanoverians for nearly a century.

In 1994, a developer purchased the Eichelberger School and converted it into professional office condominiums, re-naming it the Eichelberger Professional Building. Andy and Michael Hoffman, Hanover High alumni themselves, purchased the Eichelberger auditorium in 1997 as part of a deal to purchase five other condominiums at the Eichelburger Professional Center. In July of that same year, the Hoffmans donated the auditorium back to the community so that it could become the Eichelberger Performing Arts Center.

Today the Center is home to the Hanover Symphony Orchestra. The Board of Directors for the Eichelberger Performing Arts Center as of 1998 are: President, Richard Carson; Vice-President, Andrew Hoffman; Secretary, Matthew Guthrie, Treasurer, Linda Cole; and Financial Advisors, Karl Lehman and Rodney Roger. Completing the Board are: James Baumgardner, Lorraine Becker, Mary Ann Fiery, Estelle King, Larry Kuntz, Robin Lawrence, Nancy Leister, Jane Rice, Jessica Staub, and Robert Webb.

A one million dollar renovation campaign is currently underway. The Campaign Committees raising community support are: Corporate Gifts, Steve Harner and Larry LaMaina; Major Personal Gifts, Estelle King and Jane Rice; Community Gifts, Mary Ann Fiery and Nancy Leister ; Alumni Gifts, Myrt Small; Grants and Foundations, Linda Cole; and Special Events, Chuck Lambert and Rene Staub.

When the Hanover Opera House opened in 1887, the editor of the local newspaper reminded the townsfolks that its success depended upon their support. One hundred and ten years later those same sentiments were echoed with regards to the Eichelberger Performing Arts Center in an editorial which appeared in the July 23, 1997 issue of the Evening Sun. The editorial concluded, "Eichelberger is about history, community, and tradition. It is about the future and the hope to bring a performing arts center to our town. It is also about ownership and will only be as good as the people who support it..."

They Made the Music

After I saw the picture and read about the German Band and how it was formed, I could not resist writing this letter.

I know there are literally hundreds of musical people in and around Hanover who will agree with me. I refer to the contributions the Gobrecht family has made to music and musicians throughout the years.

I was my good fortune to be one of the many students who got their start because of the untiring and unselfish efforts of this family...

... Few towns can say they have one family which has contributed as much to music as the Gobrechts.

If kindness, unselfishness, encouragement and talent ever become the currency of the day, these men will be wealthy beyond any standard...

<u>The Evening Sun</u>
April 18, 1972
Letter to the Editor
Clyde Mummert
Gettysburg, R.D. 5

There is the inherent danger of offending someone when only a handful of personalities are selected to be highlighted from among the literally hundreds of people who contributed to Hanover's long and rich musical heritage. Those included here by no means constitute a complete listing of the musically- gifted or community- minded in Hanover. Nor are the short biographical sketches here meant to diminish the musical contributions made by others. It is not a question of inclusion or exclusion, but rather, a simple fact that without the involvement of key musicians, directors, and certain civic- minded individuals , the river of musical excellence in Hanover might indeed today flow in a different course.

Only three of the individuals highlighted claimed musical professions. The others passionately practiced their musical pursuits as an avocation. But they all shared two common denominators ; a love of music and the desire to bring pleasure to their friends and the community through their music.

Adam Ault

An erratic and somewhat eccentric Pennsylvania Dutchman, Adam Ault purchased property on the west side of York Street in 1800 on what is now Middle Street in Hanover. Here he erected a large two-story brick house and pursued his craft of building organs and harpsichords. Born in Prussia , he immigrated to Philadelphia in 1785. He lived in Bethlehem for a few years and then moved to Lititz where he learned the trade of organ building in the factory of David Tanneberger.

Ault was a skilled machinist. He spent ten years under Tanneberger's tutelage and acquired a fine understanding of the art of music. He applied a considerably high level of ingenuity in building pipe organs. One of the first pipe organs he built was purchased by the Lutheran and Reformed congregations who worshipped in the Stone Church in Codorus township. Though no exact list of how many organs Ault built exists, the number has been estimated at more than twenty.

Though supposedly a Moravian, Ault held peculiar views on religion and never visited any of the churches where his instruments were installed. Neither is there any evidence that he could claim membership in any local church. In his will he set aside twelve square feet in the southeast corner of his lot as a burial ground for himself and his family. Although the local newspaper reported that a large number of the leading citizens of Hanover attended his funeral, no mention is made of any kind of religious ceremonies having been conducted there.

Dr. M. M. Fleagle

At the time of his death on May 30, 1944, Dr. Maurice Monroe Fleagle was one of Hanover's oldest and most respected physicians. He was one of the local pioneers in the establishment and advancement of X-ray therapeutics. In his forty-six years of practice, he delivered over 2400 babies. In spite of his demanding medical career, he was an ardent supporter of music and community musical affairs.

He was a talented violinist who in his later years became a musical director. Testaments at his death eulogized that the main incentive for his musical pursuits was to help the community develop a real appreciation for the best in music.

He was a founding member of the Beethoven Club of which his sister-in-law Charlotte C. F. Hauser served as president for many years. He formed Fleagle's Parlor Orchestra, a 24 piece group of which he was the director. The orchestra eventually evolved into the Hanover Civic Orchestra. He served as the Hanover Civic Orchestra's first conductor. Upon his retirement in 1939, he was named Conductor Emeritus.

Dr. Fleagle took in concerts and operatic performances wherever he traveled. He frequently attended performances at the Lyric Opera House in Baltimore.

Viola Brodbeck Fleagle

By many accounts, Viola Brodbeck Fleagle possessed one of the most beautiful soprano voices to ever grace a stage in Hanover. She was a popular soloist with the Hanover Civic Orchestra and in the local churches, especially at Trinity United Church of Christ where she was a member. Mrs. Fleagle's vocal expertise reached well beyond the Hanover borough limits.

She graduated in 1909 from Hood College in Frederick, then known as the Woman's College, and began singing in the Pennsylvania Cautauqua Circuit. Receiving highly favorable reviews at the time for the magnificence of her voice and her interpretation of the music, she traveled to Philadelphia where she studied voice professionally. While there she became a soloist with the Philadelphia Symphony Orchestra.

In 1913, she was invited to the home of then-Secretary of Labor William B. Wilson as a guest with her parents, Andrew R. and Ellen Thoman Brodbeck. Her father was a member of the US House of Representatives from Pennsylvania at the time. She sang several selections that evening for the entertainment of the dinner guests including President Woodrow Wilson.

The wife of Dr. M. M. Fleagle, she and her husband were among Hanover's most talented musical couples. She died May 30, 1944 in the same York St. home where she was born.

J. Frank Frysinger

It has been said that a prophet is not without honor save in his own country. But, Hanover held her native son J. Frank Frysinger in its highest regards. Mr. Frysinger was an outstanding organist and pianist who published more than 200 organ, piano, and vocal compositions. Local papers continued documenting his accomplishments even after he had moved out of the area.

Although known by many as a York resident, Frysinger was born in Hanover on April 7, 1878. He was the son of Jesse and Sarah Frances Sleeder Frysinger. He began to study music at the age of 8 under the tutelage of Frederick W. Wolff in Baltimore. Prof. Wolff was the organist and choirmaster of the Episcopal Protestant Church in Baltimore and director of the Haydn Oratoria Society in Hanover. He studied with several other concertmasters over a ten year period including Richard Burnmeister, the last pupil of Franz Liszt and court pianist to the Emperor of Germany.

During the early 1900's Frysinger played extensively in the Hanover area, serving for five years as the organist for the Emmanuel Reformed Church. The local papers carried rave reviews of his artistic capabilities anytime he gave a recital or concert with the Beethoven Club or Concordia Club.

Frysinger made his concert debut in 1907 as a touring concert soloist and was featured at the Jamestown and

Philadelphia Sesquicentennial Expositions. He headed the organ department at the University of Nebraska School of Music from 1911-1919. He also served as head of the organ and theoretical department at Augustana College Seminary, Rock Island, Ill. Concruent with these positions he served as organist and choir director at the First Presbyterian Church in Lincoln, Nebraska and St. John's Methodist Church in Davenport, Iowa.

From 1942-1952 he taught in the music department at York Junior College. He died In 1954 in York, PA, and is buried there in the Prospect Hill Cemetery.

Edward J. Gobrecht

Edward J. Gobrecht was a self-taught musician who in turn became one of Hanover's most prolific musical instructors. He was often referred to as "Hanover's Music Man ". Born in Union Township, Adams County, he was the son of John A. and Emma Stonsifer Gobrecht. He was a descendent of the Rev. John Christopher Gobrecht, the first member of the Gobrecht family to come to America in 1753.

His idol was Trombonist Arthur Pryor and although he could play all the brass instruments, he specialized in the trombone. His music achievements were so numerous that the following is only a representation of his involvements.

He was the director of the Knights of Pythias Band and continued as director when this band evolved into the Moose Band of Hanover. He was a member of the six Gobrecht Brothers Orchestra and Hanover's Little German Band. He served as director of the orchestra and singing for St. Paul's Lutheran Sunday School in Hanover for 38 years. At the same time he held the position of director of the William F. Myers Son's Band in Westminster, MD, for 27 years. He also served as the director of another half-dozen bands in York County. He played the violin and trombone for the Hanover Civic Orchestra and played trombone for five years with the York Symphony Orchestra.

On May 9, 1960 the Hanover Senior High School Band honored him with a plaque in recognition for his years of service to music in the community. Edward J. Gobrecht taught more than 1000 pupils in his career and filled the ranks of local high school bands and orchestras.

Emma Stonesifer Gobrecht

Although she never lived in Hanover or belonged to any local musical organization, Emma Stonesifer Gobrecht made an immeasurable contribution to the town through the encouragement she gave her children to pursue their individual interests in music. Emma Gobrecht was the wife of John Andrew Gobrecht and their union produced 12 children- 6 boys and 6 girls. Raised on the family farm in Union Township, just east of Littlestown, the six boys- Levi, William, Emory, Clayton, Edward , and Joseph- became the instrumental music directors, performers, and teachers of their day.

By all accounts, Emma Gobrecht was a woman of many talents. She possessed a natural ear for music and could reproduce a song on her parlor organ after hearing it played just once. Her father, Jacob Stonesifer, taught music in the public schools of the day, but Emma received no formal musical training.

These are the six Gobrecht brothers with their instruments in 1912. As grown men, these six sons of John A. and Emma Goebrecht would become the leaders of instrumental music in Hanover for more than fifty years. Standing in the back are: Levi, William, Emory, and Clayton while Joseph and Edward stand forward. They got their musical start in the Carroll County Reed Band and four of the boys are wearing the band's uniforms.

The six Gobrecht brothers received much of their inspiration and musical ability from their talented mother. Regrettably Emma Goebrecht never heard a performance by the Six Gobrecht Brothers Orchestra which formed in 1922. She died in January 1910 at the age of forty-four.

Emory A. Gobrecht

One of the six musically talented Gobrecht brothers, Emory A. Gobrecht directed the Trinity Sunday School Orchestra for over 30 years and served as the director of the American Legion Post 14 Drum and Bugle Corps for many years. He was employed by Hanover Shoe, Inc., for 62 years.

Emory Gobrecht served as a sergeant in the Army in WW I and was his company's bugler. He took over the job of Sunday School Orchestra director and leader for the singing at Trinity United Church of Christ shortly after returning from the war. It was Emory who instigated forming an orchestra with his brothers and made the assignments as to what instruments each brother would play.. He played the xylophone and served as leader of the Six Goebrecht Brothers Orchestra.

While never receiving any formal instrumental training, he did study musical composition under Prof. F. H. Losey, one time director of the Hanover Civic Band. He composed over 125 poems, published a series of booklets, wrote and published several marches, played in the orchestra at the Hanover Opera House, and served as the treasurer of the Pennsylvania Bandmasters Association.

Prof. Jacob A. Gundrum

Prof. Jacob A. Gundrum's name appears listed in almost every musical organization in Hanover from 1868 until his death in 1904. Most often he was designated as the group's Director.

Born in Germany, he came to the United States in 1858 and settled in Wisconsin. At the outbreak of the Civil War, he enlisted in the army and was in the Wisconsin regiments that formed the Iron Brigade. After fighting in the Battle of Gettysburg, where he was wounded in the struggle for the railroad cut on the first day, he was mustered out of the service. Rather than return to Wisconsin, he settled in the Gettysburg area for some time. He married and then moved to Hanover.

For many years he served as the director of the Hanover Silver Cornet Band. At the same time, he played in several other bands, orchestras and ensembles. Among his numerous compositions which he had published was "Recollections of Hanover". He also gave private lessons in voice and piano. In 1880, he was elected as Justice of the Peace in Hanover.

George A. Long

George A. Long was one of Hanover's best-known citizens and manufacturers. At the time of his death, he was the head of one of Hanover's largest manufacturing plants-The Long Furniture Company, makers of fine extension tables at the West End. He also owned and operated the George A. Long Cabinet Company. Here he manufactured Victrola cabinets and worked under contract producing cabinets for the Edison Talking Machines and Columbia Granfonolas.

Despite his hectic professional schedule, Long always made time for music in his life. He hosted several functions annually for both the Beethoven and the Concordia Clubs. Possessing a fine bass voice, he was a local singer of prominence. He helped to organize the Hanover Oratorio Society and the Choral Society, serving as president of these societies at various times.

He was one of the founders of the Hanover Agricultural Society and the Hanover Improvement Company. He was also one of the organizers of the Hanover Trust Company and served on its first Board of Directors. He was the younger brother of John Luther Long.

John Luther Long

John Luther Long was born at 47 Frederick St., Hanover, PA, in 1855. He was the son of Henry and Sarah Funk Long. His father was a prominent member of St. Matthew's Lutheran Church where he served as leader of their German Choir for sixty-three years.

As a young man he taught in the Penn Township schools, read law in the office of Attorney Charles M. Wolff. Later he practiced law in Philadelphia. While practicing law he wrote his famous story "Madame Butterfly". With David Belasco, he turned the story into a play which was produced in New York in 1900. His story formed the basis for the libretto of Puccini's famous opera by the same name.

Long died in 1927 in Clifton Springs, N. Y. He is buried in the Mt. Olivet Cemetery, Hanover, PA.

Clara Glatfelter Moul

Mrs. Clara Glatfelter Moul was the wife of Charles E. Moul, a prominent Hanover businessman who held interest in a number of Hanover's manufacturing plants.

Mrs. Moul devoted her time to a number of civic activities. She served as president of the Hanover Civic League, was the first president of the Visiting Nurse Association, and was one of the founders of the Hanover Young Women's Christian Association, which organized in 1920. Though no public announcement was ever made, it was general knowledge that the YWCA's building, located on Carlisle Street at that time, was a gift from Mrs. Moul.

Mrs. Moul was an active member of St. Matthew Lutheran Church and was very magnanimous in her giving there. The church's beautiful alter, the Tiffany stained-glass window in the front of the church, and the great Austin organ were all gifts from Mrs. Moul. Proceeds from a fund established by Mrs. Moul still supports the maintenance and repairs for the organ.

Mrs. Moul loved music and helped promote its development in the community. She was a member of the Beethoven Club and their meetings were often held in her town home on Broadway or her country home at Hershey's Hill.

Clyde L. Mummert

Clyde L. Mummert was a violinist and strings teacher in the Hanover Public School District for 18 years. He then joined the Gettysburg Public School staff as the strings teacher and orchestra director; a position he held for 16 years until his retirement in 1984. He was a mentor and friend to many of today's string musicians in the Hanover area.

Starting violin lessons at the age of nine, he studied music at the Peabody Institute in Baltimore, MD, and graduated from Gettysburg College. He founded the Hanover String Quartet in 1992.

A freelance musician, he played in the Harrisburg Symphony Orchestra, the York Symphony Orchestra, Frederick Chamber Orchestra, and the Potomac Symphony Orchestra. He was the principal player in the viola section of the Hanover Symphony Orchestra at the time of his death in October 1997.

Harry C. Naill

Harry C. Naill possessed an excellent tenor voice and sang with the choir of St. Matthew Lutheran Church for many years. He sang with other local vocalists Miss M. Josephine Wolf, George A. Long, and Sharon Smith. He was an instrumental figure in forming the old Choral Society of Hanover, which existed at the turn of the twentieth century.

Naill was a Justice of the Peace at the time of his death in 1952. In the early 1890's he was the office manager at the original offices of the Hanover Show Company on Railroad Street.

J. Herbert Springer

J. Herbert Springer presided over and was the father of one of the largest church organs in the world. He formulated the design of the magnificent Austin organ which was installed at St. Matthew Lutheran Church, Hanover, in the congregation's fifth church building in 1924. Over the next forty years, he would continue to make additions and enhancements to the majestic organ who's construction was made possible by a then anonymous donor. While later it became common knowledge that the organ was a gift from Clara Glatfelter Moul, even after her death in 1935, Springer maintained that her secret should be kept per se her wishes. He never referred to her by name in any publicity articles concerning the organ.

Springer began his musical life at the age of five with piano lessons in his hometown of Harrisburg, PA. At the Harrisburg Conservatory of Music, he studied piano with Miss Nellie Bennett and organ with the Conservatory's Director Edwin Decevee. He graduated from the Conservatory at the age of 13. While he had several excellent teachers in various parts of the world, Springer always credited much of his development to Tobias Matthay. Springer studied piano with Matthay in London and later applied many of Matthay's principles to his organ technique.

Mr. Springer's first organist position was at Calvary Presbyterian Church in Harrisburg in 1913. Two years later he became the organist in the Fourth Reformed Church of Harrisburg. After beginning study at Gettysburg College in 1916 with a major in chemistry, he was contacted by St. Matthew Lutheran Church in Hanover and offered the position of organist and choirmaster; a position he held for fifty-two years, until his retirement in 1968.

J. Herbert Springer, organist at St. Matthew Lutheran
Church for 52 years, was the designer of the great Austin
organ in that church. Photo courtesy of the St. Matthew
Lutheran Church Archives.

He was a faculty member of the Music Department of Gettysburg College for 15 years where he taught both piano and organ. He retired from the college faculty in 1966 but continued to teach private lessons.

Harry W. Swartzbaugh

Harry W. Swartzbaugh was born in Hanover in 1896. He was the son of John and Ida Free Swartzbaugh. He was an active member of St. Paul's Lutheran Church and director of St. Paul's Sunday School Orchestra from 1914-1925. He was also co-founder and organized of the Hanover Lyric Band. He served as the band's director for 23 years. He was a printer by profession and at one time was a chef at the former Holland Restaurant in Hanover.

Appendix I

The Bells of Hanovertown

Herbert Heath Helman

Far up on the old belfry tower,
Where as boys we spent many a Sabbath hour,
While parson preached or hearers prayed,
In the quaint old chapel of former days,
Whose rough-hewn timbers and lofty spire
Stood the shock of war and test of fire,
There, swinging with graceful ease or calmly looking
down,
Are the silver-tongued bells of Hanovertown.

Bells that have chimed their melody loud and clear,
With faithful devotion, year after year,
Bell's that have responded to their master's arm
In paeans of joy or tones of dread alarm,
Bells that have kept their long peaceful stay,
While generation after generation have passed away,
Bells that are worthy of an emperor's crown,
Are the sweet-tongued twin bells of Hanovertown.

What thrills of joy to the human heart,
Do they with their silver melody impart!
While on the still, quiet Sabbath morn,
They with their music, which seems heaven-born,
 Awake in the soul a peaceful delight,
To hope in the future, and fear not the night!
Oh! Blessed bells of cherished renown,

Bells that are the joy of Hanovertown.

Where're the wandered from the sweet spell,
Chance to pitch his tent or permanent dwell-
Be it in the peaceful quiet of rural life,
Or in the busy throng of city strife,
Or in the rosy kingdom of the Orient,
Where're thy children fate hath sent,
There, ever and anon, through the dim vista echoing
down,
Come the sweet sounds of the bells of Hanovertown.

As the incoming tide with resistless sway,
As the golden sunbeams heralding the day,
As the bright sheen of glory with silver light,
Covers the earth on calm moon-lit night,
As the note of linnet far up in the sky,
As the chorus of angels from one high,
So, abiding and sweet, is the memory of the sound,
Dear bells, twin bells, of Hanovertown.

Oh, ancient bells, of our fathers bless'd,
Hallowed by thy memory in each son's breast!
Oh, ancient bells, to our fathers dear,
May we thy sound ever love to hear.
And as age comes on with quick'ng tread,
May they sweet strains bid us not dread,
Blend thy clear notes with Heaven's sweet sound,
Dear twin-bells, sweet bells, of Hanovertown.

Appendix II

Chronology of Hanover Bands

1776-1784   Fifes, tenor drummers, and bass drummers serve with the Pennsylvania Line under the command of Brig. General "Mad" Anthony Wayne.

1812-1814   Hanover drummers and fifes served in the American Army under Generals Scott and Brown during the War of 1812.

1840-1842   Union Band. First brass band formed in Hanover under the leadership of William Bange. It disbanded with the outbreak of the Mexican War in 1846.

1852   Union Band re-organized by Capt. Daniel Albright.

1857   Hanover Brass Band formed. Musicians played silver over-shoulder instruments imported from Vienna, Austria.

1859   Citizens Brass Band organized with James Hoffman as leader. Disbanded in 1861 with the outbreak of the Civil War.

1859   The Marion Rifle Drum Corps organized from the south-central Pennsylvania area and went to war in 1861.

1860   Juvenile Cadet Drum Corps organized.

1868   Hanover Silver Cornet Band organized with Prof. Jacob Gundrum as leader and instructor.

1876   American Independence, a Drum Corps of 31 pieces, with Louis I. Renaut as Fife-Major, was organized in the Hall above the American Hotel on Railroad St.

1879   The Harmonica Silver Cornet Band organized with Frank S. Zinn as leader.

1883   Local veterans of the Grand Army of the Republic organized a Drum Corps of 16 pieces from among their sons.

1886   Citizens Brass Band organized with Louis G. Pfaff as leader and Prof. Joseph Prosho as instructor. After several years, this group merged with the Hanover Silver Cornet Band.

1888   A Juvenile Brass Band was organized under the leadership of Prof. Paul Eiserman. Later adopted the name Clipper Band until 1893 when it disbanded. Many of its members joined the Hanover Silver Cornet Band.

1896   Hanover City Band organized under the leadership of Prof. Frank H, Losey. He was also a general agent for H.N. White musical instruments.

1901   Cresent Band organized under the directorship of Prof. Emil Eiserman.

1903   Hanover Drum Band organized by the Fire Company. Initially, under the direction of Paul Eiserman.

1903   K. of P. Band organized. Consisted initially of 16
       members of the local Knights of Pythias Lodge No.
       318. In 1904 it joined with Company 7,
       Lancaster U.R., K. of P.

1910   K of P. Band officially designated as the Second
       Regiment Pennsylvania Brigade Band by Brigadier J.
       M. Reichard. At that time, it was the largest
       K of P Band in the United States with 57 members.

1913   P. O. S of A. Band organized under the direction of
       Dennis Dell. This band performed over 90
       appearances annually in the local area.

1920   Harold H. Bair American Legion Post 14 Drumand
       Bugle Corps organized.

1923   Boys Club Band organized under directorship of A.
       Balley Morelock.

1925   Hanover V.F.W. forms a drum corps.

1929   Hanover Senior High School Band organized. Its first
       conductor was Harry C. Stenger who served in this
       capacity until 1934.

1932   The Lyric Band of Hanover organized November 1st
       in the Parkville Fire Company with H. W.
       Swartzbaugh as its first conductor.

1935   By this date the Pennsylvania Brigade Uniform Rank
       Knights of Pythias Band was performing concerts
       under the directorship of Edward J. Gobrecht.

1953   Moose Band Hanover Lodge # 227 formed from the Knights of Pythias Band under the directorship of Edward J. Gobrecht.

1958   The American Legion Post 14 Drum and Bugle Corps adopts the name " Hanover Lancers ".

1961   Southwestern High School Marching Band organized under the direction of Robert Shreffer.

1963   The 130 piece Bicentennial Band, Moose Band, and Lyric Band provided nightly concerts the week of June 24th as part of the celebrations of the 200th anniversary of the founding of Hanover.

1976   Community Bicentennial celebration includes concert played byHanover's Bicentennial Honor Band saluting the five Armed Forces. The AARP Kitchen Band also performed well-known American tunes.

Appendix III

Chronology of of Hanover's Orchestras

1859-1860   Orchestra organized by Prof. James Hoffman, violinist. He also served as its first musical director.

1866   Orchestra named Free and Easy organized by Prof. Jacob Gundrum and years later played under the directorship of violinist Harry Dietz.

1870's   Several members of the Hanover Dramatic and Musical Association form an orchestra that played in the Old Concert Hall.

1872   Free and Easy Orchestra merges with the Hanover Silver Cornet Band.

1899   Hanover Philharmonic Society formed with Lewis G. Pfaff as President and C. S. McKallip as Musical Director.

1910   St. Paul's Sunday School Orchestra organized by Chester Leese.

1920   Emory A. Goebrecht appointed orchestra leader of the Trinity Lutheran Sunday School Orchestra.

1921	Hanover High School Orchestra formed with Edna Senft, Leader. Paul Gantt, the French teacher, was their advisor.
1922	Six Gobrecht Bros. Orchestra organized with Emory A. Goebrecht as director.
1925	Edward J. Goebrecht becomes leader of the St. Paul's Sunday School Orchestra.
1928	Club Royal Orchestra formed. Fronted by Guy Luchenbaugh.
1932	Hanover Civic Orchestra with Dr. M.M. Fleagle as first conductor and Walter W. Schultz as concertmeister.
1976	Robert Shrelfler directed the combined community orchestra in the Hanover Area Bicentennial Night of Music celebration held at the Sheppard and Myers Athletic Field.
1995	Hanover Symphony Orchestra formed.

Appendix IV

The following musical organizations donated their time and talents during the summer of 1997 to compile the first volume of "Christmas in Hanover". Sound Works Audio Productions, Inc. recorded selections from each group. Proceeds from the sales of the compilated recordings were donated to the Hanover Area Council of Churches. Executive Producer was Richard Carson and Music/ Mastering Engineer was Patrick F. Colgan.

Capriccio Brass

Contact: Larry Kuntz, 125 Penn St. Hanover, PA 17331 (717) 633-6720   e-mail: hanymor @netrax.net .

Duo Times Two- Mary Ann Fiery, Joan Bowman, Nancy Leister, and Joyce Elsner ** Recorded as duo-pianists.

Contact: Mary Ann Fiery, 385 Barberry Dr. , Hanover, PA 17331 (717) 632-2128.

Lyric Band of Hanover

Contact: George Rutledge, 221 George St., Hanover, PA 17331 (717) 637-2939.

Hanover Community Singers

Contact: Scott G. Fredericks, St. Matthew Lutheran Church, 30 West Chestnut St., Hanover. PA 17331 (717) 637-7101.

Hanover Standardbred Barbershop Chorus

Contact: Clair Hewitt, 114 Maple Ave., Hanover, PA, 17331
(717) 637-4574. The Whippersnappers- Contact: Michael J.
Chrismer, 5 Orin Ct., Hanover, PA 17331   (717) 633-6984.

Hanover String Quartet

Contact: Charmain Noel, Rd # 6, Box 6066 Acorn Rd.,
Spring Grove, PA 17362 (717) 225-7414.

Hanover Symphony Orchestra

Contact: Larry Kuntz, 125 N. Penn St., Hanover, PA, 17331
(717) 633-6720   e-mail: hanymor @netrax.net .

Trinity Bell Ringers

Contact: Karen L. Buckwalter, Trinity United Church of
Christ, 116 York St., Hanover, PA, 17331 (717) 637-2233.

Recorded and Produced by: Sound Works Audio
Productions, 134 Baltimore Street, Hanover, PA, 17331
(717) 632-3941.

Bibliography

Articles

"Austin", The Diapason, January 1, 1932, p.15.

Ehrehart, Amelia Melsheimer. History of Hanover, PA. Articles and Notes Pertaining to Local History. "Old Concert Hall Amusement Center," and "Pinafore", pg. 10-13, pg. 42 43 .

Program for the Dedication of the John Luther Long Tablet. The Beethoven Club of Hanover, April 4, 1948.

Official Program of the Centennial of Incorporation of the Borough of Hanover PA with Historical Sketches. 1915.

Zarfoss, Franklin W. Index of Lutheran Churches of York County, Vol. 1., Lutheran 53, pg. 5.

Books

_____ Ed. Lancers 75th Commerative Yearbook. Hanover, PA, 1995.

_____ Ed. The Nornir 1921. Hanover High School Yearbook.

Gibson, John. History of York County Pennsylvania. F. A. Battey Publishing Co, Chicago, Il, 1886, p. 591.

Gobrecht, Emory A. Home Spun Philosophy 3,4, & 5. Emory A. Gobrecht, Hanover, 1973.

Gobrecht Family. History of John Christopher Gobrecht Family 1753-1953. Craftext Quality Books, 1954, pp. 66-68.

Gobrecht, Wilbur J., Ed. History of the John Christopher Gobrecht Family in America.

Mills, Mary Kelly and Harold Colestock. <u>Forest Park, Hanover PA. A Research Study for the Pennsylvania Room of the Hanover Public Library</u>, 1995.

Prowell, George R. <u>History of York County Pennsylvania</u>. J.H. Beers & Co. , Chicago, IL., 1907.

Weiser, Frederick S. <u>The Lutheran Church on the Conewago at Hanovertown</u>. York Graphic, York, PA.,1993.

Newspapers

Evening Herald, 1894-1930

Hanover Citizen, April 1861 - August 1877

Hanover Evening Sun, 1915-1997.

Hanover Guardian, 1828.

Hanover Herald, 1835- 1930.

Hanover Independent, 1915-1943.

Hanover Spectator, 1844-1893.

Record Herald, 1901-1930.

Pamphlets

Hays, Rev. Ellis S. <u>One Hundred and Forty-five Years- A Sketch of the Emmanuel Reformed Church, Hanover, PA.</u> , Anthony Printing Co., Hanover PA, 1909.

<u>The Golden Anniversary Book of St. Paul's Evangelical Lutheran Church, York St., Hanover PA, 1890-1940</u>.

Order Form

Fax Orders: (410) 239-1823
Telephone Orders: Call Toll Free: 1 (800) 459-4126.
On-line orders: Send e-mail request to - SAMAMM@
erols.com
Postal Orders: Pudlee Publishing, Ginger S. Myers,
P.O. Box 895, Manchester, MD, 21102, USA
    Tel: 410-374-1844

Please send _____ **copies of:** Hanover Harmonies
@ $14.95 per copy

                                    Total   _____

** A portion of the sale proceeds of this book
will be donated to the Hanover Community Singers **

Sales tax:
Please add 5.00 % for books shipped to Maryland
addresses.

                              Tax   _____

Shipping:
$4.00 for the first book and $2.00 for each additional
book

                         Shipping   _____

                    Order Total   _____

Ship to:
Company name:_____
Name: _____
Address: _____
City: _____St.: _____ Zip: _____

Payment: _____ Cheque _____ Money Order

Call toll free and order now